Building a Homeschool One Room At A Time

Teaching with Mary's Philosophy and Using Martha's Methodologies

Carrie De Francisco

Outskirts Press, Inc.
Denver, Colorado

Building a Homeschool One Room At A Time
Teaching with Mary's Philosophy and Using Martha's Methodologies All Rights Reserved
Copyright © 2007 Carrie De Francisco
V2.0

Outskirts Press
http://www.outskirtspress.com

ISBN-10: 1-4327-0126-6
ISBN-13: 978-1-4327-0126-0

Outskirts Press and the "OP" logo are trademarks belonging to
Outskirts Press, Inc.

Printed in the United States of America

To Jesus Christ,
The foundation of my life

And to my husband, Michael,
For building, decorating and fixing our home
In which we live, love and learn,

And to my children, Francesca and Joseph,
For filling the rooms of our home
With laughter and precious memories.

This Book Is Not:

- a curriculum or a list of what should be taught.
- how to teach reading and math facts.
- how to teach art or music when you draw stick people and can't carry a tune.
- how to motivate your child to compose a creative story instead of watching TV.
- or which curriculum is best for each of your children.

If you are a mom whose desire is to build hearts and a home for Jesus Christ, then this book is for you.

This Book Is For:

New Homeschooling Moms

For mothers who are beginning their homeschooling journey or for moms who are thinking about homeschooling their children, this book will give some helpful insights into the day and the life of a homeschooling family. Deuteronomy 6:6-7 speaks of teaching our children about God as a on going, daily activity. *"These commandments that I give you today are to be upon your hearts. Impress them on your children. Talk about them when you sit at home and when you walk along the road, when you lie down and when you get up"*. It is my prayer that a mom new to homeschooling will read this book and have a better understanding of homeschooling, that it involves so much more than "teaching the academics". If we are homeschooling for God's glory and in God's way, then homeschooling is a lifestyle. It is a lifestyle of loving God and each other, it is living for God and in service to others and it is learning about God and what His will is for our children.

Seasoned Homeschooling Moms

This book can also be beneficial to seasoned homeschooling moms. For those of us who are now in the homeschooling trenches, we know that homeschooling is God's calling for our lives and we are committed to educating our children at home. However, with every new adventure, there comes a time when the adventure turns somewhat into a venture and then into a laborious task done with lots of venting. Educating our children at home is an awesome privilege, a blessing and a responsibility. And sometimes this monumental task can be overwhelming, draining and quite stressful. For those seasoned moms who need some refreshment and refinement, reading this book may help remove any bitterness or weariness you may be harboring. *"The Lord is my shepherd, I shall not be in want. He makes me lie down in green pastures, He leads me beside quiet waters, He restores my soul. He guides me in paths of righteousness for his name's sake"* (Psalm 23:1-3). It is my prayer that this book will help lead you to quiet waters and will make you lie down in green pastures. If it is a change of pace, adjustment in your teaching philosophy or modification in your curriculum you are looking for, keep reading. This book discusses ways to alter your homeschooling to a more gentle, eclectic and relaxed approach to teaching. It also presents new ideas to help solve old and repetitive problems that occur while educating your own at home.

Moms in General

And mothers who are not homeschooling, it is my prayer and hope that you, too, can use the ideas discussed in this book to help you build hearts and homes for Christ. *"Sensible children bring joy to their father; foolish children despise their mother"* (Proverbs 15:20). Even if you are not homeschooling, you can still reclaim, readjust and redecorate your life to make more time and space available for Jesus and for more precious family time.

How To Use This Book

Building a Homeschool, One Room at a Time, is written so that an individual can read it as part of her devotional time or as a jumpstart to her homeschooling year. It can also be used in a small group setting. It is my prayer that small group discussions will lead women to edify each other in their motherly role and to lift each other up in their homeschooling journey.

There are three sections at the end of each chapter to help you meditate on God's Word, encourage you to start a few new projects and refine your goals and objectives for homeschooling. The focus of the first section, Mary's Meditations, is on personal goals. This section offers opportunities for personal reflection time, daily devotions, and bible study questions to assist you in your personal growth and walk with the Lord.

The focus of the second section, Martha's Projects, is on family goals. It gives you hands-on projects and activities you can do to improve your homeschooling and family time. It gives ideas on how to build family relationships and how to reorganize your home.

The focus of the final section, Master Teacher's Lesson Plans, is establishing goals for your children. This section concentrates on the spiritual, mental, physical and social development of the children you are raising and educating.

Whether you are a Mary or a Martha, we are all moms in this together. It is my goal that we will support and help each other in this monumental task and awesome privilege. It is my prayer that the thoughts and ideas in this book will help you build a homeschool, one room at a time, for the glory of God. It is my prayer that the activities in this book will assist you in building hearts and homes for Christ. May God richly bless your building process and your homeschooling journey!

"Then choose for yourselves this day whom you will serve…
But as for me and my household,
we will serve the Lord."
Joshua 24:15

Table of Contents

Introduction

My Journal

As my eyes open, I notice the time. It is 5:30. Bummer! I over slept again! I usually pop out of bed around 5:00 to do my morning devotions. Well, better late than never! After a quick shower, I sit on my comfy couch to start my day with the Lord. This is by far the best part of my day. The kids are still sleeping and the house is quiet and peaceful. I love my couch. It is soft, cozy and situated in such a way that I can watch the sunrise from my back window. Today, I am studying Psalm 127:1, "Unless the Lord builds the house, its builders labor in vain. Unless the Lord watches over the city, the watchmen stand guard in vain." As I am memorizing the verse, the timer rings. Oops! I almost forgot the fresh banana bread baking in the oven. It is now 6:30. I better hurry so I can make it to the gym before the kids wake up. After my workouts, I always feel refreshed and ready to tackle the day's lessons.....

It is now 7:30 and I am home from the gym. As I am reviewing our lessons for the day, my youngest sneaks up behind me and says, "Boo!"

"Hey, handsome! How did you sleep?

"Real good, Mommy? How about you?" he replies with a smile.

"I slept like a baby. Thanks for asking." Just then, my daughter walks into the room dressed and ready for the day.

"Good morning, Mom. My bed is made and my teeth are brushed."

"Thanks, honey. Let's sit down and eat some breakfast."

My husband walks into the dining room ready to eat as well! My daughter sets the table while my little one gets the napkins. My husband pours everyone fresh squeezed orange juice and places the cups on the table while I am slicing the homemade banana bread I prepared this morning.

"Let's pray and do our family devotions."

The kids enjoy breakfast and bombard us with questions about the scripture passage my husband read. After we eat, the kids clear their plates while I get our schoolwork ready.

"Gotta go to work. See you later this afternoon." My husband kisses each of us good-bye.

"Alright, kids, let's continue reading Genesis 10 to start our lessons." We are using the bible as our history and science textbook this year. Last week we studied physics, geology, botany, zoology, astronomy and human anatomy while reading about creation and the Flood. We are now moving on to architecture and the laws of motion while studying the Tower of Babel.

As usual the kids are full of insightful and curious questions. We have fun building different towers out of blocks, marshmallows and toothpicks, straws and paperclips and of course, out of the homemade clay I made the day before. My little one narrates to me the story of The Tower of Babel while my daughter writes her reflections about their rebellion in her journal. After bible, history, science and writing, we move on to reading and math. My little one is working on his ABC's while my eldest reads a book from the library on architecture.

For math, we pull out the Cuisenaire Rods and play fraction games while my youngest builds a few more towers with the colorful rods. After our game time, my daughter goes to her room to do some independent math work and to practice her violin, while my son and I start lunch. Ah! I love our life! I can't wait for the kids to taste the salmon cakes I make for lunch! Life just doesn't get any better than this!

Now that I have the day planned in my head, perhaps I should actually roll out of bed and get my cup of coffee! Man, it is already 7:00 and I hear Joseph stirring in his room! No time for devotions or the gym and I guess we will eat those little white powdered donuts for breakfast again since I never got around to the homemade banana bread!

Reality

That is my ideal day. Now, let me share with you how our day usually goes. If I can drag myself out of bed before the kids wake up to steal some time alone with the Lord I am off to a glorious morning! If I make it to the gym at all that week, I am on a roll. And if my family actually eats something fresh baked out of the oven for breakfast, I must have had a moment of clarity and a surge of energy the night before to actually plan it and prepare it ahead of time! Fresh squeezed orange juice? Never! My daughter hates pulp and my son doesn't touch the stuff! If my daughter gets dressed before 1:00 it is a good day and if my husband actually gets three sweet tender kisses on the way out the door, he is having a super special day! Devotions? Yes, we do them daily but usually ONLY when the kids are busy eating breakfast. When their mouths are full and their hands are busy, they seem to absorb the Word better. I guess in this sense our devotion time is nourishing their minds as well as their bodies!

Mary or Martha

I must confess. I am a Martha. I do have our lessons carefully written out and I do have specific objectives for the week planned in advance. I have another confession. I love checking off items on my To Do List. I love it so much, that if I accomplish something that is NOT on my To Do List for the day, I will write it down just so I can check it off! Then life interrupts MY plans and I begin to feel stressed and incompetent as a mom and as a teacher. I really hate it when our day doesn't go the way I planned it! Yes, I can be a neurotic Martha! But there is a part of me that wants to be more like Mary. I would love to hang out at Jesus' feet first thing in the morning and all day

iii

long! I would love to rely more on God's plans for the kids and me and less on my plans for the day.

On our homeschooling journey, I have met many different kinds of homeschoolers. I have noticed that some moms are definite Martha's while some moms are complete Mary's. But what really amazes me are the number of moms who want to be a little bit of both (myself included!) I have also noticed that the "Martha moms" feel guilty that they don't incorporate more creative and spontaneous ideas into their well-planned and executed lessons while the "Mary moms" feel guilty that their days are not as organized and planned out as their "Martha" friends. After talking with many homeschooling moms I have found that many of them want to homeschool with a Mary heart while using Martha's methods.

So which one are you? Are you more like Mary? Are you a people person who loves spontaneity and living each day to the fullest? Do you "go with the flow" and use "teachable moments" as they arise? Do you have a "big picture" of where you are going each week but do not worry about the details as to how to get there? Or are you more like Martha? Do you thrive on schedules, love To Do Lists, and adore written lesson plans? Does it make you nervous when details are not planned, when the house is a mess and your To Do List is unfinished? Are you a Mary who wants to be more of a Martha or are you a Martha who aspires to be more like a Mary? My best friend, who also homeschools, is definitely a Mary! Her homeschooling day is relaxed, easy going and child-centered. She goes with the flow! I would love to be more like her. I aspire to be a Mary but the reality is I am a Martha! I am the taskmaster in the family. Our day tends to be a bit more structured. I usually have a plan in mind and tend to work towards that goal. I am a "see the hill, take the hill" kind of a person. Ironically, my "Mary" friend wants to be more like me! Is it your prayer (like it is mine) to be a little bit like Mary and a little bit like Martha?

As Christian homeschoolers, we are educating our little ones at home because we feel it is God's call for our family. We also want to make our homeschooling God-centered. *"Seek first the kingdom of God and all these things will be added to you"* (Matthew 6:33). So in our hearts, we aspire to be a "Mary". We want to start our school year and each day at the feet of Jesus. Our ultimate goal is that our children grow in their knowledge of the Word of God and that they each develop a personal relationship with our Lord and Savior, Jesus Christ. In our hearts, we know that if we have accomplished this goal, our

iv

roles as parents and homeschooling moms will be honored and blessed by God.

And then creep in our "Martha" tendencies. Not only do we want our children to learn the basics but we desire that they succeed academically as well. We want our home to be clean, our tables to be adorned with nourishing food, our walls to be covered with academic achievements AND our halls to be filled with laughter. We want our lessons to be planned, our schedules to run smoothly and our home to be organized.

Several years ago, I asked myself, " Is it really possible to have a "Mary" philosophy and teach with "Martha's" methods?" It was this question that led me to delve deeper into Mary and Martha's story and to search the scriptures for ways to accomplish this delicate balance!

In my biblical search for ways to teach with a Mary philosophy using Martha's methodologies, I read a Christian classic by Robert Boyd Munger entitled, *My Heart- Christ's Home*. It was after reading this book that I began to look at our homeschooling adventure as building a home. Using the analogy of building a homeschool, one room at a time, I began to "build" and "remodel" our home (and homeschooling).

In Corinthians 3:9, Paul describes us as God's building, *"For we are God's co-workers. You are God's field, God's building."* And our home is where we build hearts for God. *"We must not hide them from their children, but must tell a future generation the praises of the Lord, His might, and the wonderful works He has performed"* (Psalm 78:4). Using a "home" analogy to describe my role as a wife, mother and homeschooler, I found my reading and searching of God's Word kept bringing me back to Psalm 127:1-2, *"Unless the Lord builds the house, its builders labor in vain."*

With a Mary heart, I am allowing the Lord to be the Master Builder of our home. And since He is the center of our home, I can teach using Martha's methods knowing my labor will not be in vain. This book is not about the perfect curriculum, the best educational philosophy, or even how to teach like a master. It is about helping each of us, the Mary's and the Martha's, to use God's blueprint to organize our lives in such a way that we can develop a Mary philosophy using a Martha approach. The ideas in this book are to help you and me build a homeschool, one room at time, God's way. Let's begin by first looking at the overall building process.

Part One
The Building Process

Chapter 1
The Contractor

These older women must train the younger women to love their husbands and their children, to live wisely and be pure, to take care of their homes, to do good, and to be submissive to their husbands. Then they will not bring shame on the word of God."
Titus 2: 4-5

Research Associate in the Field of Child Development and Human Relations (a.k.a Mom)

Last year, I received this email entitled, **The Mommy Test**. *I was out walking with my 4-year-old daughter. She picked up something off the ground and started to put it in her mouth. I took the item away from her and I asked her not to do that. "Why?" my daughter asked.*

"Because it's been laying outside, you don't know where it's been, it's dirty and probably has germs," I replied. At this point, my daughter looked at me with total admiration and asked, "Wow! How do you know all this stuff?"

"Uh," ...I was thinking quickly, "All moms know this stuff. It's on

1

the Mommy Test. You have to know it, or they don't let you be a Mommy. " We walked along in silence for 2 or 3 minutes, but she was evidently pondering this new information.

"OH...I get it!" she beamed, "So if you don't pass the test you have to be the daddy."

"Exactly!" I replied back with a big smile on my face.

Let's be honest, being a mom can be a very challenging job! And a job it is! The little girl in this story hit it on the head (in a very humorous way) the very different, God-ordained roles that mothers and fathers have. Throw in homeschooling and a whole new dimension is added to the mother equation. Several years ago, a friend of mine sent me another email entitled, **"Research Associate in the Field of Child Development and Human Relations".**

A woman named Emily renewing her driver's license at the County Clerk's office was asked by the woman recorder to state her occupation. She hesitated, uncertain how to classify herself. "What I mean is," explained the recorder, "Do you have a job, or are you just a...

"Of course I have a job," snapped Emily. "I'm a Mom."

"We don't list 'Mom' as an occupation... 'Housewife' covers it," said the recorder emphatically.

I forgot all about her story until one day I found myself in the same situation, this time at our own Town Hall. The Clerk was obviously a career woman, poised, efficient, and possessed a high sounding title like, "Official Interrogator" or "Town Registrar."

"What is your occupation?" she probed. What made me say it, I do not know? The words simply popped out.

"I'm a Research Associate in the field of Child Development and Human Relations." The clerk paused, ballpoint pen frozen in midair, and looked up as though she had not heard right. I repeated the title slowly, emphasizing the most significant words. Then I stared with wonder as my pronouncement was written in bold, black ink on the official questionnaire.

"Might I ask," said the clerk with new interest, "just what you do in your field?" Without any trace of fluster in my voice, I heard myself reply, "I have a continuing program of research, (what mother doesn't), in the laboratory and in the field, (normally I would have said indoors and out). I'm working for my Masters, (the whole darned

family), and already have four credits, (all daughters). Of course, the job is one of the most demanding in the humanities, (any mother care to disagree?) and I often work 14 hours a day, (24 is more like it). But the job is more challenging than most run-of-the-mill careers and the rewards are more of a satisfaction rather than just money." There was an increasing note of respect in the clerk's voice as she completed the form, stood up, and personally ushered me to the door.

As I drove into our driveway, buoyed up by my glamorous new career, I was greeted by my lab assistants -- ages 13, 7, and 3. Upstairs I could hear our new experimental model, (a 6 month old baby), in the child-development program, testing out a new vocal pattern. I felt I had scored a beat on bureaucracy! And I had gone on the official records as someone more distinguished and indispensable to mankind than "just another Mom."

Motherhood... What a glorious career! Especially when there's a title on the door. Does this make grandmothers "Senior Research Associates in the field of Child Development and Human Relations" and great-grandmothers "Executive Senior Research Associates?

This is so true! As women, wives, moms, and teachers, we wear many hats and we have quite a job! God's Word describes a godly woman this way:

"She is clothed with strength and dignity, and she laughs with no fear of the future. When she speaks, her words are wise, and kindness is the rule when she gives instructions. She carefully watches all that goes on in her household and does not have to bear the consequences of laziness. Her children stand and bless her. Her husband praises her: "There are many virtuous and capable women in the world, but you surpass them all!" Charm is deceptive, and beauty does not last; but a woman who fears the LORD will be greatly praised. Reward her for all she has done. Let her deeds publicly declare her praise" (Proverbs 31: 25-31).

And in Titus 2: 3-5, women are exhorted to do the following:

"Similarly, teach the older women to live in a way that is appropriate for someone serving the Lord. They must not go around speaking evil of others and must not be heavy drinkers. Instead, they should teach others what is good. These older women must train the younger women to love their husbands and their children, to live wisely and be pure, to take care of their homes, to do good, and to be submissive to their husbands. Then they will not bring shame on the

word of God."

In Genesis, God ordained the family to be the building block of society. It is through the family that our faith and godly heritage is to be passed on from one generation to the next. *" Love the Lord your God with all your heart and with all your soul and with all your strength. These commandments that I give you today are to be upon your hearts. Impress them on your children. Talk about them when you sit at home and when you walk along the road, when you lie down and when you get up. Tie them as symbols on your hands and bind them on your foreheads. Write them on the doorframes of your houses and on your gates"* (Deut 6: 5-9).

In Hebrew tradition, a child received his Hebrew heritage and claim to be a son of Abraham from his mother's side of the family. If a child's mother was Hebrew, the child was considered to be a child of God. My husband is the head of our home. We follow his lead and ultimately his plan for our family. But as the mom, it is my responsibility to execute that plan. I am the one who has daily contact and influence over our children. It is quite a responsibility and an awesome privilege! I guess you can say I am the contractor. So if I am the "contractor," let's take a look at the building plan and what God has ordained for me to do.

The Building Plan

Paul noted that Timothy had a "Greek father," yet he was also described as being grounded in the Word of God. Paul described Timothy's heart as ripe for the gospel. *"I know that you sincerely trust the Lord, for you have the faith of your mother, Eunice, and your grandmother, Lois"* (2 Timothy 1: 5). Timothy was grounded in the Word and his heart was ripe for the gospel because of his mother's devotion to God and to His Word.

In Titus 2: 5, *Homemaker* is translated as "home worker". I am to "work" on building our home and to build up my children to be men and women who love God and His Word. *God blessed them, and God said to them, "Be fruitful, multiply, fill the earth, and subdue it"* (Genesis 1:24). My "garden" is my home. I need to subdue it, fill it, and make it fruitful!

One of the first verses in the Bible to speak to me was Psalm

127:1. It became a life verse for me. After reading this verse and Joshua 24:15, *"But as for me and my household, we will serve the Lord."* I began my quest for building a home that glorified God. I began to ask myself some tough questions:

Was I building a home built on the foundation of Jesus Christ?

Was I building a home that reflected my love and faith in Jesus?

Was I preparing their hearts to ultimately receive Jesus Christ as their savior?

Was God the master planner/architect?

Was I using the Word as my blueprint?

Was I relying on the Holy Spirit to guide me and to be the mortar that keeps everything in place?

As the contractor, was I following His plans, using the best materials and workers?

Was I cutting corners, were parts of my home in disarray, needing repair or a complete overhaul?

Was it a home that encouraged my children to become godly men and women of faith? Was I preparing their hearts so that they would have a love for God, His Word and His will for their lives?

When I first became a mom, the answer to each and every question above was NO and I was reading the wrong books to boot! I threw all the secular parenting books away and I began using my bible as my #1 (and only) parent resource book! *"Wisdom is the principal thing; therefore get wisdom. And in all your getting, get understanding"* (Proverbs 4:7). I am not a biblical scholar nor am I an educational expert! I am not a super mom nor would I consider myself a seasoned homeschooler. But I would like to share in this "building process" with you. Are you ready to get dirty and do some remodeling? Let's start building a homeschool, one room at a time!

Mary's Meditations:

1. *A wise woman builds her house; a foolish woman tears hers down with her own hands.* (Proverbs 14:1)
   How am I tearing down my home? Are certain habits tearing down our homeschool?

2. *A time to kill and a time to heal. A time to tear down and a time to rebuild.* (Ecclesiastes 3:3)
   Am I building up our homeschool? What kind of words am I using? Are they words to build up and edify my family?

Martha's Projects

1. Mentally walk around your home? Draw a floor plan of your house.   Label each room and briefly list the types of activities that take place in each room?   What kinds of materials, furniture, decorations are in each room? Keep your floor plan drawing close by. You will refer to it at the beginning of each chapter.

2. Brainstorm a job description for your "job" as a wife, mother, homemaker, and homeschooling mom. Fill in the following items listed below. For fun, compare your answers to a job description in the Appendix.

JOB DESCRIPTION:

RESPONSIBILITIES:

POSSIBILITY FOR ADVANCEMENT & PROMOTION:

PREVIOUS EXPERIENCE:

WAGES, COMPENSATION and BENIFITS:

Chapter 2

The Foundation:

Jesus Christ

For no other foundation can anyone lay than that which is laid,
which is Jesus Christ.
1 Corinthians 3:11

A Father and His Son

Several years ago a wealthy widower died with no living heir to claim his fortune. The wealthy man had only one son who tragically died several years past. When the day came for his estate auction to take place, many curious neighbors and ambitious treasure-seekers came to the gentleman's home. The visitors browsed the halls in amazement at the apparent good fortune the wealthy man had had. At the appointed time, the participants were called into the great hall where many chairs had been arranged and numerous treasures were set on display. Before the Auctioneer began, she gently placed an oil painting upon the easel and announced that the first item to be auctioned was a portrait of the owner's son.

Rather surprised and disappointed, the audience sat quietly while the Auctioneer began the bidding. Seated in the far corner of the room was a friend of the family. He knew the wealthy gentleman and often played with his son while growing up. The young man made a modest living and knew he could never afford anything that once belonged to old widower, but it had been awhile since he had been in the house. His curiosity got the best of him so he decided to come.

The Auctioneer started the bidding at $100. There were no takers. The silence was uncomfortable for the young man as the Auctioneer continually dropped the price but to no avail. No one seemed interested in purchasing the painting. Since the young man had considered the son to be his friend, he raised his hand. The Auctioneer said, "Twenty-five dollars, Going once! Going twice! Sold to the young man in the back! After the gavel hit the podium, he noticed the Auctioneer began taking down the portrait along with many other items behind her.

She looked up and said, "Thank you for coming. The Estate Auction is now finished."

The crowd began to murmur. Finally someone shouted, "What about the rest of the estate?"

The Auctioneer coolly stated, "According to the owner his most treasured possession was his only son. His son tragically died several years ago when he sacrificed his life to save the life of a friend. The father said that who ever loved his son would purchase his portrait at any price. It was the owner's wishes that, who ever purchased the portrait of his son, would also inherit the rest of his estate. This young man bought the painting so he, too, received the gentleman's entire inheritance."

What a beautiful illustration of God's love for his only begotten Son, and what a beautiful reminder of how much we have to gain if we, too, love and devote our lives to His Son, Jesus Christ. What seemed worthless to most people, the portrait of the son, was actually the most valuable item in the home! The father was essentially saying, "If you are a friend of my son, then you are a friend of mine!" And what seemed so simple to the young man, purchasing a simple painting, turned out to be the most important decision of his life. The old man blessed him with his entire inheritance just because he loved his son!

"Not everyone who says to me, 'Lord, Lord,' will enter the kingdom of heaven, but only he who does the will of my Father who is in heaven. Many will say to me on that day, 'Lord, Lord, did we not prophesy in your name, and in your name drive out demons and perform many miracles?' Then I will tell them plainly, 'I never knew you. Away from me, you evildoers!' Therefore everyone who hears these words of mine and puts them into practice is like a wise man who built his house on the rock" (Matthew 7: 21-24).

Sand or Rock

Living in Southern California where earthquakes are common, I understand how important the foundation is to the stability of a home. Our first step in building a strong homeschool, one room at time, is building our home on a firm foundation! Jesus told a parable of two men. One foolishly built his house on sand while the other built his house on rock. *"The rain came down, the streams rose, and the winds blew and beat against that house; yet it did not fall, because it had its foundation on the rock. But everyone who hears these words of mine and does not put them into practice is like a foolish man who built his house on sand. The rain came down, the streams rose, and the winds blew and beat against that house, and it fell with a great crash"* (Matthew 7:25-27).

Before we can choose the "perfect" curriculum, buy the lasted technology, or organize our daily schedules, we need to make sure our home is built on solid ground. Is Jesus Christ the center of your life? *"We are his house, built on the foundation of the apostles and the prophets. And the cornerstone is Christ Jesus himself"* (Ephesians 2:20). Is Jesus Christ the foundation on which you build everything else? *"Therefore everyone who hears these words of mine and puts them into practice is like a wise man who built his house on the rock"* (Matthew 7: 24). Is God's Word the basis for all of your decisions and choices as a family?

The answer to these questions should and must be a "Yes" if our desire is to build a home that glorifies God. I must admit my heart wants to shout out a resounding "Yes" to each of those questions but in reality, I slip in one area or another each and everyday. However, I have given my life to Jesus and accepted Him as Lord over my life so

11

I know He is the foundation of my home (and my heart). My prayer for you and for myself is that we will seek the Lord's will each and every day and rely on the Holy Spirit's guidance and strength to build and reinforce our "foundations" each day. If you have built your foundation on Jesus but perhaps your foundation has a few cracks, it is my prayer that this book will help you fill in the gaps.

What if in your heart you honestly answered "No". Jesus is not the foundation of your life. Or perhaps you are not sure and didn't know how to answer. For me I grew up in a religious home. I attended church every Sunday with my family. I was involved with the youth group. I even attended a Christian school. I knew about God but I didn't KNOW God. I grew up hearing about Jesus but I had never made a personal commitment to Him. I had never asked Him to come live in my heart and to be Lord and King over my life.

When I was pregnant with my first child, I began to feel little tugs on my heart. I wanted to share with my daughter my faith and my religion but I began to realize I really didn't have much of a faith to share. I had plenty of religious traditions and rituals I could pass on to her, but I didn't have a life saving, on-fire devotion and love affair with Jesus. I owned a bible but I never really read it. I relied on Sunday sermons to teach me what I needed to know. One day I opened my bible and began to read it for myself. The Holy Spirit began to open my heart and make each passage I read come alive! I couldn't put my bible down! I couldn't get enough of God's words for me! It was if the passages were written just for me. I finally realized just how much my Heavenly Father loved me.

The next step was finding a church that taught the Word of God! I remember walking into a gym filled with folding chairs and a handful of people joyfully greeting each other. It wasn't what I was used to. There were no stained glass window, no pulpits, and no pews but there was lots of noise! It wasn't quiet. Weren't you supposed to be quiet in church? I was greeted by many people and befriended by one woman who asked me to sit with her and her family. It was a bit awkward, but I sat down and braced myself for a "church" experience that would be quite different from what I was used to.

What happened next changed my life! The pastor walked up to the microphone wearing a Hawaiian shirt and announced that the Praise Band would not be leading worship today. The sound system was down. He informed us we would sing acappella from the hymnal. I was relieved when he said we would sing "Amazing Grace". I heard this one before but quite honestly only at funerals. I was intrigued. As we began to sing, it was like I was hearing the song for the very first time! The lyrics jumped off the page and pierced my heart! What a wretched soul I was! Tears began streaming down my face and I began to realize that not only did God love me but that He died for me. For the first time in my life, I realized what a sinner I was and that I needed Jesus! On my own, I had made a mess of my life. I needed Him and the best part was He wanted ME! That day before the preacher even began to speak, in my heart I confessed my sins and asked Jesus to be my Lord and Savior. From that day forward, I was saved. My life was changed forever!

How do you know if you are saved? First you need to realize the problem: God is a holy God and man is sinful. *"For all have sinned and fall short of the glory of God"* (Romans 3:23). Not one of us deserves forgiveness, mercy or eternal life. *"The wages of sin is death, but the free gift of God is eternal life in Christ Jesus our Lord"* (Romans 6:23). We all have sinned (rejecting God and His will for our lives). The results of which are death and an eternity separated from God. Since God is Holy, there can be no imperfection in His presence. But death was not God's plan for us. Abundant and eternal life is what Jesus came to bring. Why? Because even though man was broken and earth was filled with evil, God never stopped loving us. Romans 5:8 declares, *"But God showed His great love for us by sending Christ to die for us while we were still sinners."*

None of us are perfect. James 2:10 states, *"For whoever keeps the whole law and yet stumbles in one point, he has become guilty of all."* Even if we haven't committed murder or adultery, sin is sin to God. We could never pay our debt. Only Jesus can bridge the gap between a Holy and Righteous God and sinful man. *"If you confess with your mouth, 'Jesus is Lord,' and believe in your heart that God raised him from the dead, you will be saved"* (Romans 10:9).

It is our faith in Jesus Christ that saves us, not what we do or not do. *"God saved you by His special favor when you believed. And you can't take credit for this; it is a gift from God. Salvation is not a reward for the good things we have done, so none of us can boast about it"* (Ephesians 2:8-9). You can't earn a gift – it's an unmerited favor. You do, however, have to make the choice to accept it.

So, we all, as sinners, have to turn to God for forgiveness of sin, and trust that Jesus died to give us new life that we may be born again. It is your acceptance of God's gift; your admission that you are a sinner, your repentance (changing of your mind), and your faith in the real-but-unseen Lord is all that can bring eternal and abundant life.

Jesus said, *"I am the way and the truth and the life. No one comes to the Father except through me"* (John 14:6).

If knowing about Jesus has stirred your heart to hear more and to receive forgiveness for your sins take a moment to pray. Let God know how you feel. Pour out your heart to Him. Tell Him you are a sinner and you need His mercy and strength! Then open up your bible, get a pen and begin to learn from the Master!

The Master Teacher

As an educator, I am familiar with educational jargon. As a new teacher, I was assigned an inspiring master teacher who advised me and helped transform me into a competent and confident teacher. After many years of teaching, I became the master teacher who was responsible for teaching the new teachers how to manage their classroom, design creative lesson plans and engage the learners in meaningful ways.

Jesus was a master teacher (a rabbi) and is THE Master Teacher. As home educators, Jesus is not only the foundation of what we teach but He is also an example of how we should teach. Jesus was a model teacher. He could engage every kind of learner. *Large crowds followed him wherever he went – people from Galilee, the Ten Towns, Jerusalem, from all over Judea, and from east of the Jordan River"* (Matthew 4:25).

He knew his subject matter backwards and forwards. *"The people were all so amazed that they asked each other, 'What is this? A new teaching--and with authority!'"* (Mark 1:27). He used storytelling and concrete models to explain a difficult concept. *"Jesus always used stories and illustrations like these when speaking to the crowds. In fact, he never spoke to them without using such parables"* (Matthew 13:34). He implored large group discussions as well as small group and one-on-one instruction. *"One day as the crowds were gathering, Jesus went up the mountainside with his disciples and sat down to teach them"* (Matthew 5:1). *"Six days later Jesus took Peter, James, and John to the top of a mountain. No one else was there. As the men watched, Jesus' appearance changed"* (Mark 9:2). He consulted his "handbook" before teaching. *"In all your ways acknowledge Him, and He shall direct your paths"* (Proverbs 3:6). And before teaching, He began his day with quiet, personal prayer time. *"One day soon afterward Jesus went to a mountain to pray, and he prayed to God all night"* (Luke 6:12). He truly was a Master!

Not only does Jesus teach us how to teach but He is also the ultimate teacher of our children. *"All your children shall be taught by the Lord, and great shall be the peace of your children"* (Isaiah 54:13). What a relief that is! Knowing that God will show us what to teach, how to teach and ultimately that He is the teacher of our children can and should give us great peace! We can confidently choose our curriculum, design our lesson plans and create our daily schedules. He is in control. We can take our lead from Him. He will show us what needs to be done and when. The key is going to Him for guidance, tutoring, and trouble-shooting. *"But seek first his kingdom and his righteousness, and all these things will be given to you as well"* (Matthew 6: 33). As the contractor of this building process (mom), the foundation is set. It is set on our Lord and Savior, Jesus Christ. Now, let's move on to the first room of our house, the Living Room.

Chapter 3

The Living Room :
Intimacy with Jesus Christ

"But the Lord said to her, "My dear Martha, you are so upset over all these details! There is really only one thing worth being concerned about. Mary has discovered it – and I won't take it away from her."
Luke 10: 41-42

The "One" Thing

We first meet Martha while she is frantically preparing her home for a special dinner party. Jesus is on His way to her home for some R & R. We also meet Mary, her sister, for the first time in the gospel of Luke. While Martha is anxiously cooking and cleaning, Mary is sitting in the middle of the Living Room at Jesus' feet. She is mesmerized by her Lord and her Teacher! There is no other place she would rather be. I do believe the Living Room was Mary's favorite room to be!

Many of us (especially the Martha's), tend to empathize with Martha's frustrations. But in all honesty, I don't think Mary meant to be inconsiderate. I think Mary couldn't think of anything else she would rather do than to spend precious time at the feet of her Savior! Mary was concerned with the most important thing- spending time with Jesus! And where did Mary spend her time with Jesus? In the Living Room of course!

When my husband and I were married, we decided that we would never have a room in the house that we did not use. We wanted to make sure our "living room" was lived in! As newlyweds, we couldn't afford to not use every square inch of our home. But most importantly, we wanted our living room to be a place that was welcoming to friends and family. We wanted it to be a room that was inviting to our family! A place that was comfy and cozy and used!

A dear friend of ours has a beautiful living room. The furniture is exquisite, the fabrics are rich, and the paintings are stunning. The floor to ceiling windows invite such warmth into the room and every little nook and cranny is filled with delicate antiques. My friend designed her living room to be a special place for friends and family. A retreat area to relax, kick your shoes off and catch up with old friends. It is a room that invites you to stay a while. What a wonderful idea! A room set aside for intimate conversations and heart-warming fellowship! This beautiful room, however, is gated off to the rest of the home and the gate only comes down for special occasions.

What does your Living Room look like? What takes place in it? Is the Living Room in your home "off limits" or open to all? What makes it that way? Do your children feel comfortable and want to stay awhile or do friends feel a bit awkward and uncomfortable in this room?

Spending Time With Jesus

What does your Living Room have to say about our relationships with our family, our friends, and most importantly, our relationship with Jesus? It is natural for us to want to spend time with people we know and like. Do you know Jesus enough that you desire to spend as much time with Him as possible? John was considered the "beloved one". What did John do to in order to know Jesus so well? He ate with Jesus! He learned from Jesus! He talked with Jesus! In other words, he spent LOTS of time with Jesus! *"We are telling you about what we ourselves have actually seen and heard, so that you may have fellowship with us. And our fellowship is with the Father and with his Son, Jesus Christ"* (1 John 1:3).

If the Living Room is the place we go to spend time with people we love, is there a place for Jesus in our "living room"? How would Jesus describe your "living room"? Is it a place you go to talk with him, to share your thoughts, hopes, and worries with Him? Does He feel at ease in your living room and do you visit with Him often?

For me, I love to do my devotions in the morning on my favorite love seat. It only has room for two! I like to envision Jesus sitting next to me sharing with me a cup of coffee. My cozy love seat is in the middle of the house, so I pass it often throughout the day. When I am finished reading and praying, I usually place my bible on the empty cushion to remind me to visit with Jesus throughout the day. Every time I pass the love seat, I see the bible on the empty cushion. It is a visual for me to stop and converse with Jesus as I go through my day.

Not only is it important for me to have quiet, personal time with Jesus but my children need to see me having personal time with Jesus. They need to see that it is a priority. I also want them to see that my time with Jesus is not only precious but fun for me too! During breakfast or while we are playing, I like to share with them what I am learning during my prayer time. Many times, I will ask them to hold me accountable for the things God is asking me to do (or not to do!)

Children need to see our Heavenly Father as someone who wants to spend time with them too! Jesus loves us so much that He can't take his eyes off of us. We are the apples of His eye and He calls us friend. *"He shielded him and cared for him; he guarded him as the apple of his"* (Deut 32:10). John 15:15 states it this way, *"Instead, I have called you friends, for everything that I learned from my Father I have made known to you."*

If your children are older, encourage them to have their own personal devotional time with the Lord. Make a point to ask them what God is teaching them during the week. Ask them how you can pray for them!

"Visit" the Living Room often together. Pray about everything and all day long! Last summer, the heat was unbearable! It was extremely hot and humid but my three-year old son really wanted to go for a walk! So early that morning, my son and I ventured out into the scorching heat! Within minutes we were drenched with sweat but my son wanted to continue. As we were trenching up the hill, a cool breeze swept through the trees and brushed his little cheeks. He stopped dead in his tracks and said, "Thank you God for the wind!" My heart leaped for joy! Not only did my son acknowledge that the wind was a gift from God on this hot day but he stopped to thank Him for it! I think he praised God because we as a family stop during the day to praise God for His continually blessings. Throughout the day talk often about God's faithfulness and how He answers your family's prayers! When they come home from activities, ask them how God had blessed their day. Make sure they stop to thank God for those blessings. *"So then faith comes by hearing, and hearing by the word of God"* (Romans 10:17).

Another way we spend time at Jesus' feet is by having family devotions. The hardest part about having a family devotion time is getting started! Our family devotions are during breakfast. We keep it simple! We read a passage from the bible. My youngest narrates to us what the story or passage was about and my eldest tries to explain what lesson we can learn from it. As a family, we talk about how we can be more like the person in the story or how we can obey the commands given in the scripture. We talk about our day's schedule and how we can apply the scripture we just read to our daily activities. Then I pray for each of my children (and for myself). I make the prayers specific to that day and to the passage we just read and discussed.

Building a homeschool, one room at a time, begins with our time alone with the Lord. Our number one priority should be for us as moms to spend more quality time fellowshipping with our Lord and Savior. Let's hang out with Mary for a while and spend some time cleaning out our own "living rooms".

Mary's Meditations:

1. When do I have my most cherished time with Jesus?

2. What distractions prevent me from spending time with Jesus?

3. What can I do to make sure I make time for Jesus?

4. What can I add, remove or "clean" in our Living Room to make it a place that points my children and others to Jesus Christ?

5. How can I make it more accessible and friendly to my family and visitors?

Martha's projects:

1. Look at your To Do List (or your daily planner). Write an appointment time with Jesus and KEEP IT!

2. After your devotion time, make a point to share with your family something you learned.

3. Write a scripture verse that really spoke to you on three different post-its. Stick one on the mirror in your bathroom. Place another one by your kitchen sink and the third one by your front door. Every time you see the passage, read it, and pray it back to God!

4. Pray about everything and all day long! Create a Faithfulness Journal. Buy one of those old fashion composition notebooks and record your family's prayer requests. When God answers them, don't forget to record how and when!

5. Start Family Devotions this week! Pick a day this week to read a bible story at breakfast! Don't stress or plan too much! Pray before you begin and watch the Holy Spirit do His thing!

Master Teacher's Lesson Plans: Spiritual Goals

Write down the names of each of your children. Prayerfully consider how each child is progressing in each of the areas listed. After praying for and about each child, list your spiritual goals for this child and specific ways you can help him grow in his love, knowledge and walk with the Lord.

1. Describe your child's spiritual life.

2. Does my child have a personal relationship with Jesus? Is he/she walking with the Lord?

3. Describe your child's attitude toward church, devotional time, or other spiritual activities.

4. Does my child have a daily, personal prayer time with the Lord? Personal bible study time?

Chapter 4
The Dining Room:
Entertainment

"Do not love the world or the things that belong to the world. If anyone loves the world, love for the Father is not in him. Because everything that belongs to the world-- the lust of the flesh, the lust of the eyes, and the pride in one's lifestyle--is not from the Father, but is from the world. And the world with its lust is passing away, but the one who does God's will remains forever.
1 John 1:15-17

I come from an Italian family and I married an Italian man! For an Italian, the Dining Room is very important room. If you have an important announcement, you make it during dinner. If you have a confession, you come clean at the dining room table. If you have a problem, you ask for advice over a home-cooked meal. As a child if I were in trouble, I usually found out about it at supper. In an Italian family, most of life's issue are brought up and solved during a meal! In all honesty, I am a bit surprised that our Lord was not even a little bit Italian. He shared His innermost thoughts, gave his best sermons, rebuked his followers and enemies and even reconciled with friends over meals!

If the Dining Room is place we come to nourish our hearts and minds, let's take a look at what kind of nourishment we are "feeding" our families and ourselves. So what does your Dining Room look like? What takes place in it? Does it contain a beautiful oak table with delicate yet well-worn placemats? Or is the table filled with clutter and in-progress projects? Is your Dining Room used daily for family meals and conversations? Or perhaps, you can't remember the last time the entire family sat down together to share a blessing and meal?

Studies show successful families do three things together: eat, pray and camp together! I personally would add, play together to the list! For our family, we have 3 out of the 4. We eat, pray and play together. We slack on the camping. (This is my fault. My idea of camping is a night at the Ritz Carlton with a mint on my pillow!) Let's now turn our attention to this very important room in the home.

You Are What You Eat

We are affected by what our hearts crave and we crave what we feed on! *"Above all else, guard your heart, for it affects everything you do"* (Proverbs 4:23). Jesus describes a person's heart this way, *"A good person produces good deeds from a good heart, and an evil person produces evil deeds from an evil heart. Whatever is in your heart determines what you say"* (Luke 6:45). If we are what we "eat", let's take a hard look at what are we "feeding" our families? One of my dad's favorite expressions was "Garbage in, Garbage out!" And "What goes in must come out!" So what kind of "food" are you feeding your family?   Are you nourishing their hearts and satisfying their cravings?   Are you serving nutritious morsels of "food" to tantalize their taste buds and to develop their culinary appetites? Or are you serving nothing but "junk"? Are your cabinets filled with the finest ingredients or with worldly "junk food"?

My family's standard for choosing the type of "food" we feed our minds is Philippians 4:8, *"And now, dear brothers and sisters let me say one more thing as I close this letter. Fix your thoughts on what is true and honorable and right. Think about things that are pure and lovely and admirable. Think about things that are excellent and worthy of praise."*

Good, Better, Best

My daughter came home one day and announced that she watched an "off limits" TV show at a friend's home. My daughter knows it is a show we don't watch in our home. It isn't full of sex, violence and drugs. It is a relatively harmless sitcom but it depicts teenage girls as ruthless, clueless and obsessed with their appearance and popularity! They spend the entire half hour discussing their boyfriend troubles, their latest purchases at the mall and what so and so was wearing in Chemistry class. I sat down with my daughter and asked her what she thought of the show. I was pleasantly surprised at what she said.

"Mom, it was kind of silly. It was about a bunch of teenagers worrying about who was wearing what and who was going out with who and I couldn't tell who was friends with who. Everyone seemed to be gossiping about each other."

So I asked her if she would like to watch the program again. She promptly replied, "No, thanks. I have better things to do!" End of discussion! Apparently I didn't need to scold her for not calling and asking my permission and it didn't seem like I needed to defuse any misconceptions about the "life and times of a teenager".

If we keep our standards high, our children will raise the bar as well. In our home, Philippines 4:8 is our standard for entertainment and what we "feed" our minds and hearts. I like to stress that there are choices we can make. We can choose things that are good, better or best! For instance, the sitcom my daughter viewed wasn't necessarily bad. There was no cursing, no nudity, and no violence. Was it better than watching some horror flick? You bet! But was watching the show the best use of her time? Could she have chosen something better? Yes, Ma'am! When our family is choosing what to read, watch or listen to, I like to remind them of Philippians 4:8 and Colossians 3:2, *"Set your mind on things above, not on things on the earth"*.

I want to surround my family with beautiful things to look at, read about and listen to! We crave what we like and we like what we develop a taste for! I want to help my children develop a love for pure and lovely things. I want them to crave honorable and noteworthy things. Why show them cartoons when I can share with them my love for artistic masterpieces? Why listen to rap music while exercising when we can listen to Bach or Beethoven? Why read dawdle and fiction about aliens and monsters when I can introduce them to some of my best friends in literature. I can choose to share with my family good things like encouraging them to read a book in lieu of watching TV. Or I can go one step better and give them one of the classics to read. Or I can choose the best for them and read a classic, like the Bible, aloud together. All three are wonderful choices. The first choice can be pure (depending on the book being read). The second choice can be honorable and lovely but the final choice far out ways the first two! It is the best use of our time. We are choosing to "feed" our hearts with the best!

My son LOVES watching the Food Network! Not only is this a bit unique for a young boy but it is extremely interesting for my son, Joseph. Joseph doesn't sit still to watch anything on TV. He doesn't watch movies, cartons, sports programs, nothing! Well, except the Food Network that is! When he was an infant, guess what I watched while I nursed him in the evening. You guessed it! The Food Network! His fascination with cooking and the culinary arts per se is due largely by my addiction to Emeril Live and 30-Minute Meals! Not that these are bad shows to watch but in hindsight, I could have chosen a better use of my time while nursing my son. Just think what "culinary appetites" I could have instilled and developed in him if I would have chosen the "best"!

What's For Dinner?

The first step in preparing nourishing "meals" for our children is to let our children see us choosing godly entertainment. Before we can set a "nutritious and lovely" meal before our family, we need to make sure we are "eating" a healthy diet. Our choices need to be the "best"! So what kinds of choices are you making? What is on your menu of "desires"? What type of entertainment do you watch? What kind of music do you listen to? What kind of books do you read? *You may say, 'I am allowed to do anything.' But I reply, 'Not everything is good for you.' And even though I am allowed to do anything, I must not become a slave to anything*" (1 Cor. 6:12). Our habits (especially bad ones) can cause our little ones to stumble. "*But if anyone causes one of these little ones who trusts in me to lose faith, it would be better for that person to be thrown into the sea with a large millstone tied around the neck*" (Mark 9:42). Sure, we have freedom in Christ, but are the things I am choosing to do helping my walk with God? Are my choices becoming stumbling blocks for my children, family and friends?

In order to build a homeschool, one room at time, our next step in this building process is to evaluate how we spend our time. Let's face it. What our children fill their minds with during playtime will find its way into your school time- for better or for worse! I am almost positive Martha spent a lot of time in the Dining Room. She probably prided herself on the lovely and pure meals she served her family and guests. Let's take a hard and honest look at our "dining rooms" and what we are "feeding" our family. Let's cook up a meal Martha would be proud of!

Mary's Meditations:

1. What of the "world" is in my home? Is there enough evidence in your life and in your home to "convict" you of being a Christian?

2. What is important to you?

3. When you have some down time, what does your mind wander to? Is it lovely? Honorable? Righteous?

4. Are there any activities you do (or your family does) that you would not feel comfortable inviting Jesus along? What entertainment is (or can be) a stumbling block for your family?

5. What can you add, remove or "clean" in your Dining Room to make it a place that points your children and others to Jesus Christ?

Martha's Projects:

1. Children need to see you choosing godly entertainment. Brainstorm your favorite TV shows, radio stations and authors. Highlight the ones that would make God proud. Cross out the ones that would make Jesus blush or turn in disgust. Make it a goal to eliminate at least one of the crossed out items from your daily activities this week.

2. What are you allowing your children to watch, read and listen to? Walk around your home and pray in each room. Ask God to show you what "idols" and "worldly treasures" are in each room. Pray for the courage to eliminate those things!

3. Think about the past two weeks. List the number of evenings you ate together. If it is at least 10 out of 14, pat yourself on the back! If it is 7 or less, list the reasons, activities and interruptions that occurred that kept you from sharing a meal together. Pick one to eliminate this week. Prepare your family's favorite meal (and dessert) and serve it on that night! Set the tone by playing inspirational or classical music in the background.

4. Brainstorm all of the activities in your life and your children's life. Pray over which ones can be eliminated to make room for more family time and quiet time. Make an effort to eliminate at least one from each person's list.

5. Instigate Family Night! It can be anything- a family hobby, game night, weekly devotional time, movie night, a special dinner- anything that brings the family together at least once a week. Put it on your calendar! Mark it in red on your husband's calendar! Guard this night!

6. What was your favorite literature book when you were a kid? Check it out at the library and read it to your kids THIS WEEK!

7. Go outside this week with your family and take a Nature Walk! Enjoy God's beautiful creation together!

Master Teacher's Lesson Plans:
Fine Arts and Physical Goals:

Write down the names of each of your children. Prayerfully consider how each child is progressing in each of the areas listed. After praying for and about each child, list your fine arts and physical goals for this child and specific ways you can help him grow in the gifts, talents and interests the Lord has placed in his heart.

1. Does my child have a special talent or gift? What is it? What am I doing to encourage and help develop this God-given talent?

2. Does my child have an interest or hobby that occupies his/her thoughts and time? Is there a class or mentor I can find to help enrich this passion in my child?

3. Is there an interest or hobby that occupies his/her thoughts and time that is not "pure and lovely"? How can I eliminate this "worldly" interest?

4. Is there a museum, magazine or group we can subscribe to as a family to further develop his/her interests or gifts?

Chapter 5

The Study:

Education Learning

Keep a close watch on yourself and on your teaching. Stay true to what is right, and God will save you and those who hear you
1 Timothy 4:16

When my husband and I first got married, we spend many hours negating each other's actions. Each morning after I got out of bed, I would turn on all the lights in the kitchen and would begin to make a pot of coffee. My husband would enter the room and turn off the overhead light and the light by the sink leaving on only the small counter light. Being a newlywed, I smiled and waited for him to leave the kitchen and then I would promptly turn back on all the lights! I couldn't see, I couldn't concentrate, and I hadn't had my cup of coffee yet! I liked the bright lights cascading throughout the room. It helped awaken my senses.

After drinking my cup of java, I would go to the bedroom to get dressed. Each morning the sunshine shined through the open shutters, but the room was still very dark and somewhat dreary. So, I would promptly flip the overhead light switch, make my way to closet and proceed to flip the light switch on in the closet. Who can make a decision on what to wear if you can't properly see the clothes you are looking at! I often heard a little "humph" from my darling, young husband who would then patiently wait for me to retrieve an outfit from the closet. Then without warning as I was barely out of the closet, he would abruptly turn the closet light off, meander out the room and causally flip off the overhead light of the bedroom as well as he exited the room. Of course, this left me alone in the "dark" again to get dressed!

This went on for months. In the back of my mind, I was thinking he was such a penny pincher! I know things are tight and we need to be frugal with our money, but can't we use the electricity! Later on I found out my husband was thinking the opposite of me. It drove him crazy. He felt like every light in the house was on at the same time (which of course it wasn't. Only the room I was in was filed with light!) He thought I was being wasteful and I thought he was being cheap!

Then I began my Master's program and took a class on learning styles. What an eye-opener! I leaned that not only did individuals learn in different ways but that individuals concentrated better in different environments. What? People can actually think clearer huddled over a book with only one little desk light on in the midst of a dark room? No way! But as I was reading, learning (and experimenting on my husband), I found that it was true! I needed a bright room with lots of natural and artificial light in order to concentrate and my husband worked best by the light of only one, little lamp. We have come a long way since then. I respect his need for bits of lights here and there and he patiently waits to turn off the lights in the study until I have completed all of my work. Every morning, I open all the shutters in the house while keeping all the overhead lights off during the day. At dinner, I light candles and turn on the lights in the dining room but at bedtime, only one lamp is lit while we read in bed. I appreciate his need for darkness and he acknowledges my need for light!

Now that my children are growing into their own preferred study habits, I find my daughter likes lots of natural and artificial lights when reading and doing projects and my son prefers dark corners and closed shutters! Go figure!

Fearfully And Wonderfully Made

Our foundation is firmly set on Jesus Christ! The Living Room is now being used to build intimacy with the Lord. The table in the Dining Room is being used to tantalize our family's taste buds for the good things in life- fine art, good music, classical literature, and nature's best. Now it is time to turn our attention to our home "office," the room where the majority of learning takes place. The room where new ideas are discussed and questions are asked. This is the room where new concepts are introduced and old skills are practiced. Let's now enter into the Study.

So what does your Study (or office, workroom, etc) look like? What takes place in it? Is it filled with books, games and art supplies? Are the books being used or are the supplies filled with dust? For us, the Study (or office) is literally in the middle of the house and it is where the majority of our learning takes place. The computer is in this room. Bookshelves housing hundreds of books lace the walls of this room. Our printer, fax, talking globe and CD players are scattered throughout this room. Educational toys, board games, math manipulatives, science equipment and puzzles fill the baskets and clutter the shelves in this room. Pictures, artwork, maps and charts adorn the walls as well. When you walk into our office, it is obvious we homeschool! There is not a space not being utilized and every nook and cranny is overflowing with "stuff"!

What we teach our children is extremely important, however, the way we teach our children is of equal value. Jacob also valued the importance of going at a pace his children could bear. In Genesis 33:14, Jacob pleads, *"Please let my lord go on ahead before his servant. I will lead on slowly at a pace which the livestock that go before me, and the children, are able to endure, until I come to my lord in Seir."* He knew he could only drive the children at a certain pace, a pace they could endure. He was willing to sacrifice time in order to ensure the children arrived at their destination safe and sound. This is a powerful lesson for us to learn. As homeschooling moms, sometimes we are driven by our curriculum or our state's scope and sequence instead of by the needs and abilities of the children we teach. *"Train up a child in the way he should go, And when he is old he will not depart from it"* (Proverbs 22:6). Another way to view the phrase *"to train up a child in the way he should go"* is "to teach a child to the particular bent he has". In other words, teach a child to live a godly life in a way he understands. Our children are fearfully and wonderfully made and each of them are created completely different! God created them with unique gifts and personalities. Our Creator designed them exactly the way He wants them to be so that they can grow into the person He wants them to become. God has created them special and has set them apart to do His will. It is our job as parents to patiently and prayerfully discover our child's particular God-given "bent".

Learning Modalities

"For You formed my inward parts; You covered me in my mother's womb. I will praise You, for I am fearfully and wonderfully made; marvelous are Your works, and that my soul knows very well" (Psalm 139: 13). Each child is unique and will learn in his own unique way. How your child learns, how he processes information, and how he interacts with his learning environment all have a tremendous affect on how he will process, understand, and apply the skills being presented to him. Does you child learn like Mary, Martha or Lazarus? In order to teach to a child's particular "bent," we need to take a further look at different learning modalities and learning styles.

I like to think of learning modalities as the "glue" that helps bits of information stick to a work of art. As the child is learning new information, these bits of new information are "glued" on in different ways. Learning modalities is how information is remembered or how it "sticks"! A visual learner might "glue" (or remember) the new information by using glitter glue. It is appealing and it catches the eye! The auditory learner might "glue" (or remember) the new information with a roll of tape. He can hear each piece of information being taped into place. Still the kinesthetic learner might use Elmer's glue to make the new information stick. White glue has great texture and it has a unique smell. The bottle itself needs to be squeezed and as the glue dries, the texture and color changes. Learning modalities are all about how to get new information to "stick"!

Visual Learners (a.k.a Mary)

Where did we find Mary when Jesus was teaching and talking with His followers? At His feet watching everything He did! The visual learner tends to have a "photographic memory." The visual learner will need to "see" new information in order to learn and remember it. Like Mary, help your visual leaner to get a "mental picture" of what's being taught. Draw a diagram of what is being explained. Write notes in brightly colored pens or use "flashcards" that have been written in different colors. Ask your child to rewrite his notes often. Use posters that explain procedures or better yet have him design his own posters.

Kinesthetic Learners (a.k.a Martha)

When we meet Martha for the first time, she was moving in 5 different directions all at the same time! She was moving and multitasking! When she heard Jesus was on His way to Bethany, Martha was the one who ran to meet Him. She was a woman of action. The kinesthetic learner is in constant motion! A kinesthetic learner needs to physically participate in a task and he usually needs to have some part of his body in motion while thinking. To help your kinesthetic learner retain information incorporate concrete models into his lessons. Allow him to "play" with modeling clay or "exercise" while listening. Use tactile stimulus with your learner. Make sandpaper flashcards or trace problems and answers in salt. The more he moves, tastes and touches, the more he will remember.

Auditory Learners (a.k.a Lazarus)

We do not hear much about Mary and Martha's brother, Lazarus. However, we do finally meet him ironically after he is dead and buried. Mary is watching the crowd mourn while Martha is running to meet the Lord. We read that when Jesus did arrive at the somber scene, He calls out to Lazarus and commands him to come out of the tomb. What happens next? Lazarus obeys and walks out! He heard, he listened, he understood, he obeyed! An Auditory Learner learns best through hearing! He will learn and retain more information if it is given to him orally. While doing word problems, have him read them aloud or use computer games that "talk" to him. If he is taking a test, read the questions aloud. While he is memorizing facts or new procedures, have your child read his notes aloud. The auditory learner loves books on tape. Invest in courses on video or on CD's that put facts to be memorized to music.

Learning Styles

Individuals remember information by either seeing, hearing or feeling- the three major learning modalities. The way individuals learn and process information is unique as well. Traditionally, learning styles have been categorized into four major groups. Some children are Intuitive Learners who are inspired by social interaction, stories and knowing up front why the new information is important. Some children are Logical Learners who like to learn facts in an orderly and sequential manner. Still others are more Active Learners who learn by doing and moving! Finally, some children are Innovative Learners who like to figure things out for themselves and apply their new knowledge in different ways. So what type of learner is your child?

Intuitive Learners

"For I have great joy and encouragement from your love, because the hearts of the saints have been refreshed through you, brother."
Philemon 1:7

The Intuitive Learner is a true "people person". She is motivated and encouraged by those around her. She enjoys "refreshing" others and being "refreshed". She has a big heart and genuinely wants to see those she loves happy. She is very sociable and thinks better in a harmonious environment. She likes to talk her way through a problem and tends to seek advice from others before making a decision. She wants to know why something is important first before learning about it. She loves to hear stories about real people. If this sounds like your child, then integrating literature books and biographies into your lessons is an excellent way to pull your Intuitive Learner into your unit of study. To truly engage your Intuitive Learner, first ask her personal questions before starting a new lesson and then after reading, question her about her opinions or feelings regarding the story. Given that this type of learner enjoys the company of others, enjoys helping others and likes to "talk aloud" while learning, using cooperative games to teach and review skills is also an excellent way to engage this child.

Logical Learners

"Instead, his delight is in the Lord's instruction, and he meditates on it day and night."
Psalm 1:2

The Logical Learner delights in thinking and meditating. He loves to learn new things and learning usually consumes him day and night. He values facts and figures more than feelings and opinions and views things in black and white. He prefers traditional teaching and information presented in a logical and sequential manner. He prefers to know how the "experts" solve a particular problem so that he can follow their example. He enjoys competing with others and strives to meet the goals he has set for himself. He values precision and is very conscience of details. Since Logical Learners would be considered a "traditional" student, using "traditional methods" such as workbooks and standardized tests are usually quite effective. This child also enjoys using logic and competition so employing games can be an effective way to reinforce new skills.

Active Learner

"So he jumped up, stood, and started to walk, and he entered the temple with them--walking, leaping, and praising God."
Acts 3:8

The Active Learner is too busy "living life" to stop and do book work. He learns while walking, jumping and leaping. He is a whirlwind! If you have an Active Learner in your family, there is no question as to how he learns. He prefers to move during a lesson and loves "action" projects. He wants to "do" a lesson instead of "learn" a lesson. He wants to apply the new skill in his life now and he needs to know how he can use this new information today! If this describes your child then using everyday experiences to teach and reinforce skills is the most effective strategy you can use. Get your Active Learner involved in the kitchen, the garden, and the garage. Have him build with blocks and take apart old appliances. To engage an Active Learner, do an activity first and then connect it to the facts and figures in the book later. In this way, he has tangible, first-hand knowledge of a concept that he can connect to the abstract when it is presented to him. He will learn the new skill faster and retain it longer if the new skill is approached in this order.

Innovative Learner

"A man's heart plans his way, but the Lord determines his steps."
Proverbs 16:9

The Innovative Learner spends most of her time thinking up new things and planning her next adventure. She has a list of projects and things she wants to do and try out (although her list usually isn't neatly written anywhere.) She is passionate about her passions. She likes to experiment and to test out ideas. She is a flexible thinker and a creative problem solver. She tends to be dramatic, artistic and thinks "out of the box". She is very curious and likes to take new information learned and use it in new and improved ways. Since your Innovative Learner sees things a little differently that the rest of us, she enjoys solving problems that have more than one answer or problems that can be solved in more than one way. She loves tackling brainteasers, riddles and mindbenders. When planning lessons for your Innovative Learner, make sure to plan extra time and allow her the freedom to choice how she will solve a problem or how she will present a project. She enjoys the challenge and it is a great lesson in problem solving as well.

(Learning Styles and Learning Modalities taken from *Math FUNdamentals: Storytime,* Carrie De Francisco, 2003)

Do You Learn Like Mary or Martha?

My husband and son are both Active Learners. They are in perpetual motion! They are constantly working on new projects (hands-on of course). If they are busy, then they are happy! I am Logical Learner. I like schedules. I like order. I like to learn independently. Tell me what needs to be done; I will do it quickly, efficiently and usually before the deadline. My daughter is an interesting mix of an Intuitive Learner and an Innovative Learner. She learns best when given an opportunity to explore ideas on her own but she desperately needs to run her ideas by someone. She wants someone's input before starting a project and she wants your approval after a project is completed. But don't dare give her a set of specifications for how to achieve her goal or even suggest the "best" way to accomplish her objective. She prefers to view your guidelines as mere suggestions. She is full of "what-ifs" and "Let's try this"! With regards to learning modalities, my husband and son have to move while learning, I need to see it to believe it and my daughter needs to hear it (or in most cases, sing it!)

Because of this unique mix of learning styles and learning modalities, we implore a more "eclectic" approach to homeschooling. We include a little bit of Mary, a touch of Martha and a portion of Lazarus to our learning. While studying the arts, literature and history, we move at Mary's pace. We sit and relax while we read and we talk a lot about the topic we are studying! We stop to smell the roses. We really delve deep into the topic and learn all that we can learn in a very casual way. While studying the sciences and the world around us, we move more at Martha's pace. We play lots of games and we do lots and lots of projects! We keep moving and we keep busy! We are in the kitchen, like Martha, a lot but we are usually cooking up an experiment or two instead of a meal! While learning the three 3'Rs (the basics), we move in time with Lazarus' pace. Steady, slow and methodical. This is when we break out a workbook or two. We review, memorize and practice.

Keep in mind while choosing a curriculum (if you use one at all) that your curriculum should be a *guide*. Don't become a slave to your teacher's manual. Pace your schoolwork according to the pace your children can travel. Make sure the scenery along the way is interesting and enticing. Make sure you not only teach the basics but you teach it in a way they can understand it.

Which type of learner are you? How do you retain and remember information? Chances are you learn and remember in a different way than your child. Studies suggest that teachers teach in the way they learn. You may be presenting information in a way that makes sense to you but if your learner thinks differently than you, chances are your approach and presentation isn't making sense to him!

Find out what your learning style is and then figure out what your child's gifts and interests are. God has made your child exactly the way He wants him to be. Our Heavenly Father designed your child with his unique gifts to be used for His purposes. It can be frustrating at times teaching a child who thinks differently than you do. If you don't understand his way of thinking, then your time together can become quite exasperating. *"Rejoice always, pray without ceasing, and in everything give thanks"* (1 Thess 5: 16). Rejoice always in the Lord and in the beautiful child He has given you. Rejoice in your child's strengths and gifts. Pray without ceasing to the Lord that He will give you the wisdom to discern your child's individual learning needs and give you the patience you need to work with your child's weaknesses. Give thanks to the Lord for the opportunities to teach your own child at home and the liberty to teach your child according to the way he learns.

Your child's gifts and strengths and are unmistakably from God. Make sure you allow him opportunities to explore and learn using the learning modalities that make sense to him. Encourage your child and find ways to help him develop his strengths. God may use these strengths when he is grown for His glory. *"God has given gifts to each of you from his great variety of spiritual gifts. Manage them well so that God's generosity can flow through you"* (1 Peter 4:10).

Whistle While You Work

The Study is also the room in which we teach our children the virtues of perseverance, patience, ingenuity, problem solving and the value of good-old fashion hard work. It is one thing to teach your child phonics and mathematical procedures but are they also learning how to persevere when the learning gets tough? It is one thing to teach to their particular "bent" and to encourage their strengths, but it is also important to teach them good study habits as well as good work ethics for when the going gets tough. *"Whatever your hand finds to do, do it with your might"* (Eccelassties 9:10). Paul rephrases it this way in 2 Timothy 2:15, *"Concentrate on doing your best for God, work you won't be ashamed of."*

Do your children put forth their best efforts not only in the subjects they excel in but also in the subjects that are difficult for them? One of the first bible verses I had my daughter memorize was 1 Corinthians 10:32, *"Whatever you do, do all to the glory of God."* First we brainstormed all the things she typically did in a day. We wrote everything down, from brushing our teeth to school work to hula class. In one column, we listed the things she liked to do and the things in which she excelled (hula and science were at the top of the list!). In a second column, we listed the things she did not like to do and the areas she was weak (writing and brushing her hair topped this list!) I asked her which items on the list were things she did for God. She gave me the usual responses of church, reading her bible, doing her bible study, playing with her brother (I thought that was interesting) and saying her prayers. I then told her I would highlight on her list other things she did for God. I then proceeded to highlight everything. Needless to say, she was a bit shocked.

"You mean when I am brushing my hair, I am doing it for God? And making my bed? And adding fractions too?"

We then talked about 1 Corinthians 10:32 and that EVERYTHING we do, we should do it all for the glory of God. We are to "love each other, be obedient, discrete, chaste, and hard workers so that *that the word of God may not be blasphemed"(*2 Titus 4-5). We should do our best not for the praise of men but as if we are doing it for the Lord Himself. And that includes math too!

Yes, it is important to expect the best from our children. But it is also important to extend grace as well. Are you creating an atmosphere where your children can make mistakes and learn from them or are you expecting perfection 100 % of the time? When they mess up (and as you know they will!), are you extending grace to them or are you expecting your children to act or perform as an adult?

In order to build a homeschool, one room at a time, we need to rearrange the room in which we do most of our "schooling"! In the "Study", Mary and Martha come together to work and learn side-by-side even though God gifted each of them differently. I can imagine Mary wanting to kick back, relax and read a good book while Martha was eager to finish her latest project and get started on her next entertaining extravaganza! In the Study, let's work on making Mary comfortable while keeping Martha busy!

Mary's Meditations:

1. How do I learn best? Am I an auditory, visual or kinesthetic learner? Do I teach to my particular learning modality or to my child's?

2. How can I help my child discover, build, and use his gifts? How can I help them succeed?

3. Are our studies based on biblical principles and a Christian-world view? Am I discussing with my child what the bible has to say about the topics we are studying?

4. Do I expect the best from my children and then extend them grace when they fail?

5. What can you add, remove or "clean" in your "Study" to make it a place that points your children and others to Jesus Christ?

Martha's Projects:

1. Do you expect your children to finish their homework just so they can move on to the next activity or do you insist they take their time and do their best? Show your children you value hard work and diligence by what you set aside time for.

2. Let your children see you learning a new trade or hobby. Share with your family what you are reading and what you are learning. Set aside time this week to do one of your favorite activities.

3. Ask your children weekly (or daily) what they are learning and how you can pray for them.

4. Get your child involved in a variety of activities? Find out what his strengths are and allow your child the time to pursue them. If it is challenging, don't let him give up before a class or season is over. He made a commitment. Insist he follow through.

5. Set up a time and place for schoolwork. Make sure to include Christian-worldview materials such as bibles, bible atlases, bible dictionary, Christian fiction, stories of Christian heroes, etc.

6. Check out from your local library a book about learning styles. Read it and pray for discernment with regards to each of your children.

7. Make a point this week to put away the workbooks and textbooks and go on a "fieldtrip"! Bring along your art pens and nature journal. Take along a bag lunch and plan to eat at the park! Ask your family to help you plan what you will do and where to go but then let the Holy Sprit be your Guide while at your destination. Explore and then stop to smell the roses! Then get up again and explore some more!

Master Teacher's Lesson Plans:
Academic Goals

Write down the names of each of your children. Prayerfully consider how each child is progressing in each of the areas listed. After praying for and about each child, list your academic goals for this child and specific ways you can help him develop and grow in each academic area.

1. If your child could learn one thing this year, what would you want it to be?

2. How can I incorporate my child's learning style to help him read and comprehend better?

3. How can I incorporate my child's learning style to help him problem solve and calculate better?

4. How can I incorporate my child's learning style to help him write and express himself better?

5. How can I incorporate my child's learning style to help him appreciate and explore the sciences more?

6. How can I incorporate my child's learning style to help him learn and apply lessons learned from historical events?

Chapter 6
The Kitchen:
A Servant Heart

When Jesus had washed their feet and put on His robe, He reclined again and said to them, "Do you know what I have done for you? You call Me Teacher and Lord. This is well said, for I am. So if I, your Lord and Teacher, have washed your feet, you also ought to wash one another's feet. For I have given you an example that you also should do just as I have done for you.
John 13: 12-15

Since we started homeschooling, I feel like I am in the kitchen all day long. I am up preparing breakfast first thing in the morning and then there are dishes to do after breakfast. Since we homeschool, our midmorning snack is prepared in the kitchen (and most often consumed in the kitchen as well). Then before you know it, it is time for lunch. I am back in the kitchen (or at least one of my kids are) whipping up something fast and nutritious. Then, there are more dishes to do after lunch. Around here the 4:00 munchies hit! All are back in the kitchen for some cheese and crackers (or if Joseph is in charge, milk and cookies)! More snacks and more messes to clean. This is the time of the day I am furiously in the kitchen fixing dinner. This is when the pots and pans really start to fly! I have the whole food pyramid I need to hit and all in the one meal. This takes a lot of planning and a lot of time to prepare. Then dinner is finally served. All is eaten (except for the beets my husband hid under his corn on the cob) and then, you guessed it. We are off to the kitchen one last time to clean yet another round of dishes!

Busy, busy, busy! In which room do you spend most of your time? In which room do you work the hardest? Which room seems to have a never-ending list of things to do? Which room is continually in use and continually messy? If you are like me, you most likely answered the kitchen.

So what does your kitchen look like? What does it sound like? Dare I ask, what does your kitchen smell like? What takes place in your kitchen? I mentioned earlier that I am Italian. On special occasions or holidays when family and friends came to our home to celebrate, it never failed: Everyone would congregate in the kitchen! It was the happening place to be! Now that I am the mom, I find the same phenomenon happening in our home. Whenever we have a party or dinner guests, each and every person seems to wander at some point into the kitchen! It is no wonder people gravitate to the kitchen. It is the heart of the home! If you want to talk to mom, you can probably find her in the kitchen. Why look for mom in the kitchen? Because the kitchen is where we moms serve our families best!

Server or Short Order Cook

What do we do in the kitchen? We cook, sweat, pace, clean, and in my case, complain! Much like a short order cook, we serve our family while in the kitchen and dare I say, without much gratitude or appreciation. In all honesty, sometimes I wish I could put a sign on the kitchen cabinet that says, "The cook went fishing!" But according to Jesus, the definition of service is to follow His example. He, the Rabbi and Lord, sat down and washed his disciples feet! It wasn't His job to do this and it certainly wasn't expected of Jesus to wash the disciples' feet. He did it because He loved his disciples. He wanted to serve them. Most importantly, He wanted to give them an example to follow! *"So if I, your Lord and Teacher, have washed your feet, you also ought to wash one another's feet. For I have given you an example that you also should do just as I have done for you"* (John 13: 12-15).

In Matthew 5:41, Jesus gets right to the point. *And whoever compels you to go one mile, go with him two.* Ouch! I can think of a few people right here in my own home that compel me to run a cross-country race! And my Lord wants and commands me to not go one mile but two! Dare I say the kitchen was probably Martha's favorite place to be? From scripture, it sounds like she played hostess a lot! She was used to extending a hand to her neighbors and showing gracious hospitality to strangers. We know one of her favorite guests was Jesus and from the sound of it in Luke's gospel, she desperately wanted everything to be just right for Him. Isn't that how we feel about our family? We want to serve them. We want to make them smile. We want to "wash their feet" and make them feel special. We receive so much more when we know we have given our families the best we can. *"I have shown you in every way, by laboring like this, that you must support the weak. And remember the words of the Lord Jesus, that He said, 'It is more blessed to give than to receive' "* (Acts 20:35).

Rejoice!

To be honest, I know I tend to complain and grumble like Martha as well, especially when I am in the kitchen! Sometimes, I just don't feel like serving. Sometimes, I want some help (and lots of it)! Sometimes, I would like to feel appreciated (with lots of compliments, thank you's and some flowers would be nice!) Paul summed it up nicely how to combat those pestering complaints. *"Rejoice in the Lord always. Again I will say, rejoice! Let your gentleness be known to all men. The Lord is at hand"* (Philippians 4: 4-5). What is God's will for me? *"Rejoice always, pray without ceasing, in everything give thanks; for this is the will of God in Christ Jesus for you"* (1 Thessalonians 5: 16-18).

Rejoice! That's the ticket! Ultimately, I need to remember all that I do, I do for God. Whether it is washing dishes, changing diapers, doing the laundry, or cleaning the dishes for the tenth time that day, I need to remember to "*Work hard and cheerfully at whatever you do, as though you were working for the Lord rather than for people*" (Colossians 3:23). When I am weary and tired, I need to rejoice, choose joy, smile and remember Isaiah 40:31, "*But those who wait on the LORD will find new strength. They will fly high on wings like eagles. They will run and not grow weary. They will walk and not faint.*"

When you find yourself grumbling, thank God for the opportunity He is giving you to serve Him and your family. Look at it as an opportunity to show your children by your example how to serve others with a servant heart. And when all else fails, PRAY! Love and joy can only be multiplied when you give it to others. Just like the fish and 5 loaves of bread. It wasn't until the boy gave everything he had that the Lord multiplied his offering. The Lord blessed his unselfishness. He used his servant heart to bless others! The kitchen is a wonderful place to serve our family and in the process, our children will learn through our example how to serve others!

Teach your child to have a servant heart. Do service activities as a family. Participate in holiday out reach programs. A homeschooling friend buys umbrellas and blankets in the summer when they are on clearance. During January when the rain season begins, she loads up the kids and the supplies into her car. As it is raining, they drive down a busy street in Old Town Pasadena looking for homeless individuals. Each one they find, they hand to them an umbrella and a fresh, dry blanket. Inside the blanket, she tucks away a miniature New Testament Bible for them to discover (and hopefully read). If your children are older, encourage them to help out neighbors with manual-labor chores for FREE! What a witness to your neighbors and what a powerful lesson for your child! Get the kids involved in KP duty! Start them young! Be creative! Through your example, your children will learn a valuable lesson in giving and serving others.

To Eat or Not to Eat

The godly woman described in Proverbs 31: 27, "*watches over the ways of her household, and does not eat the bread of idleness.*" As a wife, mom, (and teacher), you probably don't feel like you eat the bread of idleness. However, we do need to be weary of serving too much! For my church, I help bring meals to new moms. Our church's mission is to fill their refrigerators with homemade meals for a couple of weeks. This way the mom is free to rest and to concentrate on the new baby while the dad and the rest of the family can rest at ease knowing their needs will be meet. One evening, I was rushing out the door with a meal for a new mom. As I was leaving my youngest said, "Oh that smells good! What are we having for dinner?" I promptly answered, "I don't know but I need to deliver this before it gets cold. I'll be back in a few minutes." As I was driving in the car, I couldn't help notice the irony. A family from my church would be well fed tonight while my family would probably feast on PBJ sandwiches and boxed macaroni and cheese! I shared this event with my neighbor who I consider to be my mentor and she told me never put others before my family. That really stuck with me! So now when I am asked to prepare a meal or two for someone in need, I check our calendar and offer a day that would not interfere with my family's activities. And while I am preparing dinner for my family, I make a double batch to deliver the next day to the new mom and her family.

My husband is the one who reminds me daily to "just say no!" It isn't because he is stingy or grumpy; it is because he knows me too well! I have a hard time saying no. Now when I am asked to volunteer, participate, or lead something, I respond with "Let me pray about it, talk to my husband and get back to you!" And I do just that. I pray diligently about the request to make sure it is in God's plan for my life. I consult my husband to make sure it fits in our family's time budget and then I give my answer a few days later.

A servant heart is an honorable thing to possess, especially when we serve with the right motives and with no complaints. But it is something else to be so busy you can't keep your head above water. A friend of mine sent me this email about being too B.U.S.Y.

Satan's Meeting: (Read even if you're busy)

Satan called a worldwide convention of demons. In his opening address he said, "We can't keep Christians from going to church. We can't keep them from reading their Bibles and knowing the truth. We can't even keep them from forming an intimate relationship with their

Savior. Once they gain that connection with Jesus, our power over them is broken. "So let them go to their churches, BUT steal their time, so they don't have time to develop a relationship with Jesus Christ. This is what I want you to do," said the devil:

"Distract them from gaining hold of their Savior and maintaining that vital connection throughout their day!"

"How shall we do this?" his demons shouted.

"Keep them busy in the non-essentials of life and invent innumerable schemes to occupy their minds," he answered. "Tempt them to spend, spend, spend, and borrow, borrow, borrow. Persuade the wives to go to work for long hours and the husbands to work 6-7 days each week, 10-12 hours a day, so they can afford their empty lifestyles. Keep them from spending time with their children. As their families fragment, soon, their homes will offer no escape from the pressures of work! Over-stimulate their minds so that they cannot hear that still, small voice. Entice them to play the radio or cassette player whenever they drive. To keep the TV, VCR, CDs and their PCs going constantly in their home, and see to it that every store and restaurant in the world plays non-biblical music constantly. This will jam their minds and break that union with Christ. Fill the coffee tables with magazines and newspapers. Pound their minds with the news 24 hours a day. Invade their driving moments with billboards. Flood their mailboxes with junk mail, mail order catalogues, sweepstakes, and every kind of newsletter and promotion offering free products, services and false hopes. Keep skinny, beautiful models on the magazines and TV so the husbands will believe that outward beauty is what's important, and they'll become dissatisfied with their wives. Keep the wives too tired to love their husbands at night. Give them headaches too! If they don't give their husbands the love they need, they will begin to look elsewhere. That will fragment their families quickly! Even in their recreation, let them be excessive. Have them return from their recreation exhausted. Keep them too busy to go into nature and reflect on God's creation. Send them to amusement parks, sporting events, plays, concerts and movies instead. Keep them busy, busy, busy! And when they meet for spiritual fellowship, involve them in gossip and small talk so that they leave with troubled consciences. Crowd their lives with so many good causes they have no time to seek power from Jesus. Soon they will be working in their own strength, sacrificing their health and family for the good of the

cause. It will work! It will work!"

It was quite a plan! The demons went eagerly to their assignments causing Christians everywhere to get busier and more rushed, going here and there. Having little time for their God or their families. Having no time to tell others about the power of Jesus to change lives. I guess the question is has the devil been successful in his schemes? You be the judge!!!!! What does "BUSY" mean? B-eing U-nder S-atan's Y-oke

Paul writes in Timothy 5: 13-15, *"Besides, they are likely to become lazy and spend their time gossiping from house to house, getting into other people's business and saying things they shouldn't. So I advise these younger widows to marry again, have children, and take care of their own homes. Then the enemy will not be able to say anything against them. For I am afraid that some of them have already gone astray and now follow Satan."* We don't want to be so busy that our servant heart turns into a sour heart- a heart full of bitterness and grumblings! Sometimes we load up our days (or in my case the mini-van) with so many things to do, that our load gets too heavy and burdensome. *"Come to me, all you who are weary and burdened, and I will give you rest. Take my yoke upon you and learn from me, for I am gentle and humble in heart, and you will find rest for your souls. For my yoke is easy and my burden is light"* (Matthew 11: 28-30).

In order to build a homeschool, one room at a time, we need to de-clutter our kitchen! We need to look at serving our Lord, Jesus Christ, through service to our family. We need to examine our "overloaded day", remove what keeps us too "B.U.S.Y" and replace it with Jesus' yoke and will for our lives. Martha is ready and waiting for you! Let's get cleaning!

Mary's Meditations:

1. Who in your home is easy to serve? Who in your home is hard to serve?

2. What responsibility or chore can I take over for my husband? How can I serve my children better?

3. What do you do over and over each day that drains you of your joy and patience? Do I find my job as mom, wife, home "worker" mundane?

4. Do I grumble aloud or in my heart as I do my "jobs" around the house? Do I become aggravated when I feel overwhelmed or when it seems like I am working solo?

5. What can I add, remove or "clean" in the kitchen to make it a place that points my children and others to Jesus Christ?

Martha's Projects:

1. Pick three of your favorite bible verses that encourage you. Write them on post its and tape them all around your kitchen. When you feel like complaining, pray back scripture instead!

2. Play uplifting music or Christian radio while doing usual chores in the kitchen. You might just find your children dancing (and helping) in the kitchen too!

3. Pray each morning for ideas on how to serve your husband and how you can bless your children that day. The Lord will give you plenty of ideas if you ask. Pick one idea and do it TODAY!

4. Go on a prayer walk around your neighborhood with your children. Bake cookies for an elderly neighbor. As you go on your prayer walk, stop to visit with an elderly neighbor. Make sure to give him your fresh baked cookies!

Master Teacher's Lesson Plans:
Work Habit & Character Goals:

Write the names of each child. Prayerfully consider the work habits and character traits of each child. After praying for and about each child, list ways you can help him develop and grow in responsibility and service to others.

1. Does my child cooperate with a happy heart? Is he a team player at home and with his siblings?

2. Does my child express gratitude when others serve him?

3. Does my child take responsibility for his chores? Does he take the initiative to do his chores without being reminded?

Chapter 7
The Family Room:
Relationships

For where your treasure is, there your heart will be also.
Luke 12:34

Treasure Island

The story, *Cornelius' Jewels*, is a Roman folktale about a mother and her two children. As the story unfolds, a very wealthy friend visits a peasant woman. The ostentatious friend brings with her her finest jewels to show her poor friend. After the wealthy Roman visitor has shown each of her prized possessions, she asked her peasant friend, "And what precious gems do you have to share?" Much to her surprise, the young mother responds saying she has a treasure far more precious than the woman's jewels. In disbelief, the older woman demands that she present her treasure before her. The young mother gently places her arms around her two sons and says, "This is my treasure. My most precious gems. There is nothing more important to me than my sons!"

I like to think of our Family Room as an island with several different wooden treasure chests just waiting to be filled with precious "treasures"! A place to kick back, relax and have fun! I want to fill it with gems of laughter and with precious memories. I want my children to know they are my "precious gems" and I want my children to view each other as priceless treasures to each other. God first and then family! After our relationship with God, there is nothing more important than our relationship with our family! I want my kids to have fond memories of growing up. I pray that my children will be best friends now and as adults! I want them to value our family and our times together as a priceless treasure! *"Finally, all of you be of one mind, having compassion for one another; love as brothers, be tenderhearted, be courteous"* (1 Peter 3: 8).

No, our Family Room isn't decorated with a tropical theme nor does it look like Treasure Island, but it is the one room in the house where no shoes are allowed! In order to enter, you must kick off your shoes and you must expect to relax and have fun! This is where we play together! Pray together! Read together! Dance together! Worship together! The most precious commodity we can give our family is the gift of time!

Family Traditions

We have several family traditions but one of my favorites is the tradition of serving beignets on Christmas morning. I was born and raised in New Orleans and grew up eating (more like inhaling) beignets. Beignets are fried, French donuts that are covered with confection sugar. They are best enjoyed when delicately dunked in a steaming cup of coffee. I moved to Southern California shortly after graduating from college. Much to my dismay, the only time I could eat and enjoy New Orleans style beignets was when I baked them myself! Early in our marriage, I began making beignets on Christmas morning. It was a way for me to remember my family back home during the holidays and a way to preserve a part of my heritage. Now beignets are a favorite on Christmas morning. My husband and kids look forward to beignets almost as much as opening the presents under

56

the tree! It's tradition. It is a priceless gem I have placed in their treasure chest of memories and it is something I hope my children will continue to do with their own children.

Other traditions in our family include reading the bible story on Christmas Eve, making and opening Easter Resurrection Eggs during the season of Lent, and writing "Thanks for giving" cards to teachers, relatives and friends at Thanksgiving time. My personal favorite is our birthday dinner. When we celebrate a birthday in our family, the birthday person selects his or her favorite meal and dessert to be served on their special day. We invite grandparents and a special friend. The table is set with the fine china and the "you are special" red plate adorns the place setting of the birthday person. Before feasting on the special birthday meal, we say a blessing over the birthday person in which we thank God for that person and we ask God for his favor on his or her life the following year.

Traditions are what we do so that our children have something to look back on, to cherish, and to pass on to their children. Make your home a place your family wants to come home to. Make it inviting! Fill it with classical music, beautiful art, scriptures on the wall, and of course, the smell of fresh baked cookies! *By knowledge the rooms are filled with all precious and pleasant riches"* (Proverbs 24:4).

We are steadily building a homeshcool, one room at a time. It is time to turn our attention to the Family Room. Let's begin filling it with *"beautiful and precious things"*. Fill it with pleasant riches and fond memories. Let's fill it, physically and spiritually, with things that will point you and your family to Christ! In the time of Mary and Martha, the "family room" was located outside on the rooftop. Here they could escape the heat and the pressures of the day. They could gaze up into the night sky and talk with each other about their hopes and dreams. As sisters, they probably shared many of the same dreams and desires. I can almost see them spending endless hours on the rooftop with their brother, Lazarus, sharing their concerns and their dreams for the future. I can almost see the little wooden treasure chest in the corner of their humble abode!

Mary's Meditations:

1. Do I make my husband feel like a priceless jewel or do I make him feel more like a "diamond in the rough?"

2. Do my children feel like they are my "most precious treasure"?

3. What treasures are you storing up? What would your husband say is your most prized "treasure"? What would your children say you "treasure"? And are they the same things?

4. Are you building memories and family traditions? What traditions will you start?

5. What can you add, remove or "clean" in your Family Room to make it a place that points your children and others to Jesus Christ?

Martha's Projects:

1. Make your home inviting! Bake a fresh batch of homemade cookies today! Don't forget to dunk them in a cold glass of milk!

2. Set aside time each week for each of your children! Let them know you cherish and treasure them. List your children. Next to each name, write a day of the week next to it. On that day, go for a walk, play a game or cook dinner with that child.

3. During your quiet time, write a letter to each of your children. Tell them what you love most about them. Tell them what you pray for concerning them. Tell them a fond memory of your childhood and then tell them a funny story about their childhood. Save it and give it to them at a later date!

4. Take it a step further and start a scrapbook or something similar for each child. It can be as simple or elaborate as your time and talent will allow!

Master Teacher's Lesson Plans:
Social & Relational Goals

Write down the names of each of your children. Prayerfully consider how each child is progressing in each of the areas listed. After praying for and about each child, list your social and relational goals for this child and specific ways you can help him develop a better self-image and better relationships with siblings and friends.

1. Describe your child's personality. List his strengths and weaknesses.

2. Describe how your child relates to others.

3. Does my child know and believe he is made in God's image?

4. Does my child accept the way God made him and appreciate that God made him exactly the way he is suppose to be?

5. Does my child feel loved and accepted for who he is in our family unit?

6. Does my child love and accept others? Does my child love his siblings the way God loves him?

Chapter 8
The Bedroom:
Marriage

Then the Lord God said, "It is not good for the man to be alone. I will make a helper who is like him...".
Genesis 2: 18, 21-24

My husband is constantly working on some kind of home improvement project. Usually, he has a new project planned in his head long before he announces to me what his new venture will be. So when my husband says, "You know, I have been thinking..." I smile and brace myself for any and every possibility. It should have been no surprise that our bedroom was next on his list! The children's rooms were freshly painted, the kitchen was retiled, the living room had new lighting and the bathroom was completely remodeled. Of course our bedroom would be next on his list of projects to do. I know he does beautiful work but I still felt I needed to ask what he was planning to do to my favorite room in the house. He smiled and said, "It is a surprise!" It took every ounce to control the Martha in me and to just say, "Go for it! I can't wait to see it!"

He barricaded the room during the first day so I couldn't sneak a peek. By the first night, most of the painting was complete. As I crawled into bed, I was pleasantly surprised that he picked my favorite color for the walls. The room had such a soothing and relaxing feel to it now. It was amazing what a little paint could do. I was excited and couldn't wait to see what he was going to do the next day. The second day, he was busy cutting and sanding in the garage and hammering in the bedroom. When he reached the finishing touches, he enlisted the help of the kids. They wouldn't let me in the room. I heard "Oh's" and "Ah's", whispering and lots of giggles coming from my bedroom. They were finished and it was time for the unveiling. My husband made me close my eyes and the kids led me by the hand. When I opened my eyes, I couldn't believe it!

My husband and I went to Hawaii on our honeymoon and I absolutely fell in love with Hawaii and its aloha spirit. My husband knows how much I loved our time together in Hawaii, how much I fell in love with the tropics and how important "our space" was to me. So he turned our simple master bedroom into a Hawaiian Haven specially created for the two of us! He redecorated the room with a tropic theme right down to the pillows on the bed and the hand painted palm tree on the wall! He rehung our engagement and wedding photographs on the walls, added crown molding to the ceiling and placed a picture of the two of us on our first date on my dresser! It was now truly our special place. A space we could come to that was all ours. A place we could reminisce about our past adventures, talk about our present situations and plan our future. I was overwhelmed by the details and the amount of love that went into this project. I had tears in my eyes as I said, "I love it, Honey!"

Married With Children

So what does your Master Bedroom look like? Is it a place filled with reminders of your commitment to each other or is overflowing with clutter and "stuff"? What takes place in your bedroom? Intimate talks or conversations filled with frustration? When we first had children, our alone time together was very limited. Once we started homeschooling, it was very difficult to not talk about school-related problems and discipline during our "little talks" at night. After kids and homeschooling, what was the first thing to go? For us, it was spending quality time together. Instead of whispering sweet nothings to each other late at night, I was quickly hashing out reading problems and curriculum concerns with my husband before the snoring chorus began!

The best gift we can give our children is a loving, supportive and joyful relationship with our husband! Our children need a sense of love and security! According to recent studies, the number one worry in American children is losing a parent or the fear of their parents divorcing. When we were first married, my husband and our marriage were my first priority (after my relationship with God, of course). Our relationship needs to stay first! In my "job" description, *wife* is first! In eighteen years or so, the children will leave our nest to start families of their own, but my husband and I will remain. He needs to be my best friend as well as my husband and soul mate. And my children need to see how much our relationship and friendship means to us. It is my number one goal to act like friends and talk like friends, especially in front of our children. *"So the Lord God caused a deep sleep to come over the man, and he slept. God took one of his ribs and closed the flesh at that place. Then the Lord God made the rib He had taken from the man into a woman and brought her to the man. And the man said: This one, at last, is bone of my bone, and flesh of my flesh; this one will be called woman, for she was taken from man. This is why a man leaves his father and mother and bonds with his wife, and they become one flesh"* (Genesis 2: 18, 21-24).

Make sure your bedroom is your "haven". NO business stuff, no clutter, no checkbook registrars. Place his favorite scented candle next to the bed. Hang pictures of the two of you on the walls. Place reminders of your love and commitment to each other around the room! My husband and I have date nights. It is a priority and nothing interferes with them! If you don't already go on "dates" with your husband, start! Make them a priority! They are sacred and nothing should interfere! And don't forget those intimate moments! Show him he is still the number one person in your life. Save some energy for him!

Is There a Leak in Here?

Is it constantly raining in your neighborhood? Is there a leak in your home? Or perhaps there is a deluge cascading through the ceiling? *"A quarrelsome wife is like a constant dripping on a rainy day"* (Proverbs 27:15). The New King James Version phrases it differently. *"A NAGGING wife is like a constant dripping on a rainy day"* Proverbs 27:15 (emphasis given by me).

I know I don't nag. I just constantly remind my husband of the same thing over and over again until he finally listens to me. (Alright. I confess. I nag!) As my husband and I mature in our marital union, I am learning to take my complaints to the Lord! If I've got something to say, I try to vent it to God first and then after much prayer and a "timeout", I share my concerns with my husband! It is important we respect our husbands in public and most importantly in front of our children! I try not to complain or gossip about my husband either! *"A gentle answer turns away wrath, but harsh words stir up anger"* (Proverbs 15:1).

If you don't already, start praying for your husband. You can't be angry with someone you are praying for. When you feel like nagging or complaining, list his "negative" traits that are driving you crazy. Then begin to pray about them one by one. Ask him daily if there is anything you can do to make his day a little easier. *"She will not hinder him but help him all her life"* (Proverbs 31:12). When I am really mad at my husband, I cook his favorite meal. The old saying is true (at least for my Italian husband). A way to a man's heart is through his stomach! Taking the time to prepare his favorite meal helps me focus my attention on him and not on my "issues". I even try to set a beautiful table, complete with candles and flowers. If I am really mad at him, he gets dessert too! If you don't already, start praying for yourself! Forgiveness and change can only begin with you and with your own attitude! I must admit it is my attitude, tone or bitterness that creates tension between my husband and me. *"And be kind to one another, tenderhearted, forgiving one another, just as God in Christ forgave you"* (Eph. 4:32).

Start praying for your children's future spouses! It is never too early! Children use you as their standard of measurement for their future spouses. The kind of person their spouse will be, the values their spouse will have, and how your grown children will relate to their future spouse depends a great deal on how your children see you and your husband interact. *"Wives, be submissive to your husbands, as is fitting in the Lord. Husbands love your wives and don't become bitter against them"* (Col. 3: 18-19).

When I haul off and yell or disrespect my husband in a heated argument, I have to stop and ask myself, " Do I want Joseph's wife to talk to him the way I just talked to my husband?" Daily, I consider the possibility that my son will choose a wife that treats him the way I treat my husband. (For better or for worse!). Joyfully (or sorrowfully) Joseph will use the way I treat my husband as his model or template for his wife. On the flip side, do I want Joseph to treat and talk to his wife the way my husband treats and talks to me? (And I am blessed to be able to give a resounding "Yes" to that question!)

I consider my daughter as well when I am disputing or unleashing wrath upon my husband. Do I want Francesca to talk to her husband the way I talk to Mike? Do I want her to think this is "normal" and "godly" behavior? She, too, will look to her experiences as a child to form her model of how a wife should act! (On some really humbling days, it is scary to think she may one day act just like me!) And just as important, do I want her to chose a man who talks and treats her the way my husband treats me? The way my husband and I interact with each other as husband and wife, as co-workers, and as best friends, will ultimately effect the way our children view marriage, intimacy, relationships and commitment! It is a tough and honorable calling, but as spouses, parents and followers of Christ there is no mistake. We are called to love unconditional! *"By this all men will know that you are my disciples, if you love one another"* (John 13:35)

If you are a single, homeschooling mom, your children can learn a lot about unconditional love, faithfulness and relationships by watching how you interact with family and friends. Make sure you spend much needed time in your "haven". As a single mom, you are emotionally and physically exhausted. Make time for yourself. Actually rest and relax in your bedroom. Spend time with close friends. Venting and sharing is important. Take your concerns to the Lord and then share them with a friend over a cup of coffee. *"You will keep in perfect peace all who trust in you, whose thoughts are fixed on you"* (Isaiah 26:3).

In order to build a fruitful homeschool, one room at a time, we need to spend some quality and quantity time in the bedroom. This room is the bedrock of our school, our home, our family, and our marriage. Mary and Martha were not married but we do know that they were faithful, compassionate and respectful women. Based on God's Word, we can rest assure that they have gone down in history as disciples of Jesus. All who knew them, knew they were His because of the way they loved!

Mary's Meditations:

1. Do I make my husband a priority? Does he feel he is the most important person in my life or does he feel second best?

2. What attitude/behavior do I need to change towards my husband? What impression do my friends have of my husband?

3. When you think of your parent's relationship, what thoughts and feelings come to mind? What part of their interactions do you bring to your own marriage?

4. Do my kids know how I feel about my husband (positive or negative)? Do they know your husband is your best friend?

5. What can you add, remove or "clean" in the bedroom to make it a place that points your children and your husband to Jesus Christ?

Martha's Projects:

1. Brainstorm all the things your husband does that drive you crazy. Count the number of bad habits you listed. Now make a list of traits you love about your husband. Make sure to list the same number of positive characteristics for each negative you recorded. Get down on your knees and thank God for your husband. In your prayer, thank Him specifically for each of your husband's strengths.

2. Start praying for your husband. Write his name on a new page in your prayer journal. Start small but start today!

3. If you don't already, start praying for yourself! Write your name on the next new page in your prayer journal. List the attitudes in you that may cause or exasperate your husband's moods, feelings or reactions. Pick one you will pray about today!

4. Ask your husband if there is anything you can do today to make his day a little easier. Then do it (with a smile!)

5. Plan a date with your husband. Call the babysitter. Pick his favorite restaurant. Write him a note telling him to reserve the day! It doesn't have to be fancy. It just has to be something you put some time and effort into planning and it MUST include ONLY you and your husband!

6. Take a walk thru your bedroom. Light his favorite scented candle. Find some old pictures of the two of you and reframe them. Place them on the nightstand or someplace in your room where both of you can see it!

7. Make an effort this week to rekindle some of the physical intimacy you once shared as newlyweds. A little loving goes a long way!

8. Start praying for your children's future spouses! It is never too early!

Master Teacher's Lesson Plans:
Teaching Faithfulness

Write the names of each child. Prayerfully consider how they love and how they view faithfulness. After praying for and about each child, list ways you can help them become more loving and faithful.

1. Does my child keep his promises?

2. Does my child continually put his needs above the needs of his family or friends?

Chapter 9

The Bathroom:

Daily Confession

*But if we confess our sins to him, he is faithful and just to forgive us
and to cleanse us from every wrong.*
1 John 1: 9

I will be honest with you! I hate cleaning the bathroom! And I know there is no need to ask what your bathroom looks like and what takes place in it. We all know exactly what takes place in the bathroom! Having a young son, I am no stranger to potty talk and potty humor. And, yes, when you mention bathrooms, dirty, smelly images usually come to mind.

However, the bathroom is also one of my favorite rooms. I am not a bubble bath kind of girl but I look forward to my hot, steamy showers. When the kids were babies, I remember the worst part about my day was the fact I had no time for a shower. I remember kissing my husband hello in the evenings and promptly passing off the baby so I could finally run and take a shower!

I love showers. They are relaxing and soothing. However, I do not enjoy the soap scum that accumulates on the shower doors. It can build up to the point I can't see through them clearly. When I see the soap scum in my bathroom, I am reminded daily that the sin in my life is the same for me. Little by little, day-by-day, the sin in my life builds up. Until finally it gets to the point where I can't see clearly. With so much "soap scum" (sin), I don't view the events in my life objectively. I can't discern what is of God and what isn't. The sin scum, if you will, in my life keeps me from seeing things the way God sees them.

This is why it is so important for us as wives, parents and homeschooling moms, that we visit this "room" on a daily basis and throughout the day! *"Jesus replied, 'A person who has bathed all over does not need to wash, except for the feet, to be entirely clean. And you are clean, but that isn't true of everyone here '"*(John 13: 10). His blood has cleansed us but because of our daily and habitual sins, we are not entirely clean. We need to be bathed in His righteousness and forgiveness on a daily basis.

Mirror, Mirror On The Wall

"Mirror, Mirror on the Wall. Who's the fairest of them all?" Most evenings my answer is usually, "Not I sir!" Not because I am self conscious of my looks or because I have a poor self-image. On most days it is due to the awesome guilt trip I am having. On really bad days I condemn myself for the horrible job I did that day as a wife or mom or teacher. Sometimes, I look in the mirror and throw for myself some pretty awesome pity parties! It is during these "pity parties" I need to remind myself *"that there is no condemnation in Christ Jesus"* (Romans 8:1). I am a *new creation*! (2 Cor 5:17)

I could never image myself undergoing a facelift or a tummy tuck (I certainly could use one but let the truth be known, I am scared to death of needles!) Ah, but to get the ultimate facelift. Not the one that removes unwanted wrinkles or dark circles under my eyes or even the one that removes the extra pounds around my hips. But the "ultimate facelift" preformed by the Great Physician. *"Those who look to him for help will be radiant with joy; no shadow of shame will darken their faces"* (Psalm 34:5).

After my time with Lord, I feel radiant! After worship services and bible study, I feel bright and shiny! After a reconciliation with a loved one, I feel bright and dazzlingly! As moms, especially homeschooling moms, we need to pour out our hearts to the Lord so that no *"shadow of shame will darken [our] faces!* We need to let God transform us!

And as I leave the bathroom in my nakedness to clothe myself for the day, I ask myself what will I wear today? Paul describes the perfect, feminine outfit that any woman would be proud to wear! *"Since God chose you to be the holy people whom he loves, you must clothe yourselves with tenderhearted mercy, kindness, humility, gentleness, and patience"* (Col 3:12). Paul was quite the fashion designer! But Peter had a few fashion tips to give as well. He, too, had a few words about looking and feeling radiant. *"Let it be the hidden person of the heart, with the incorruptible beauty of a gentle and quiet spirit, which is very precious in the sight of God"* (1 Peter 3:4). Gentle? Quiet? Patient? These aren't exactly the kind of words that come to mind when describing my personality or my wardrobe, but I aspire each day to allow the Holy Spirit to renew my inner as well as my outer beauty.

Building a homeschool, one room at a time, can get quite messy! It is a dirty job but someone's got to do it! God has called you and me to educate our children at home. And we know that the teacher is going to get very dirty in the process! Pull up your sleeves. Put up your hair and let's start cleaning!

Mary's Meditations:

1. What kind of "soap scum" has accumulated in your life? What habit or "little" sin needs to be striped clean?

2. What will you put on today? With what will you clothe yourself?

Part Two
Spring Cleaning

Chapter 10
Set Up Your School Year

In the last chapter, we spent quite a bit of time with contemplative Mary. The last chapter focused on Mary's Meditations. We did some soul searching and pin pointed some personal areas that are in need of some overhauling. I can almost see Martha pacing right about now. Our action-oriented Martha is dying to get busy! To the Marys out there, it is time to roll up our sleeves and start to sweat! This part of the building process may be a bit taxing for you. If you are a true Mary, you are great with big ideas and visualizing the perfect home and the perfect school day. But the follow through can be hard! Don't get overwhelmed with the ideas in this chapter. They are merely suggestions and ideas to try.

For the Marthas out there, you are probably tired of thinking and brainstorming and you are ready to do something concrete! To my Marthas, don't go overboard (admit it, you always do!). Take the ideas and suggestions in this chapter piece by piece. It took God six days to create, Solomon several years to build the temple and Noah over 50 years to build the ark! Take your time!

In this chapter we will focus on Martha's projects. First, we will take a look at planning our school year and then we will move on to organizing our home (and homeschooling). Now it's time to get down and dirty!

One of my dear friends gets completely overwhelmed with the first step- planning the school year! The task seems so daunting and so big! How will I know if I am teaching the right things in the right way in the right order? Planning your entire year is quite simple if you start at the bottom and work your way up.

1. Choose your curriculum
2. Plan the year
3. Create a schedule
4. Generate Lists
5. Prioritize and Simplify

Choose Your Curriculum

Choosing curriculum should start in the Living Room not in the Study. Pray first about your concerns, goals and needs for the year. Make sure your agenda is in line with God's agenda for you and for your family. If you are looking for a structured curriculum, ask God to lead you to the one that will be the best fit for your family. He will be faithful to bring people into your life, ideas into your head and catalogs into your mailbox! Narrow down your choices to two or three and spend some time praying over them. Ask for God's wisdom to help you discern which way to go!

If you do not use a curriculum, pray for creative ideas and topics you and your family can study that will help your children grow in their walk with the Lord and to develop their academic skills. Check your decision with your husband. Make sure he agrees. Many times my husband will remind me of a particular area that needs to be addressed that I mistakenly left out. And many times, his ideas are more creative than mine!

Our family utilizes a little bit of Mary and a little bit of Martha in our "curriculum" choices. For the basics, we usually use a workbook type of approach. We do a little reading, writing and math every day. For our history and fine arts curriculum, we use a LOT of discussions and literature books. It is "planned" but we go with the flow and take detours when inspired to take the road less traveled. And for the sciences, we experiment, create, observe and go for lots of walks!

Our family loves unit studies! Unit studies lend themselves

nicely to using a little bit of structure and a little bit of flexibility. They are a wonderful way to incorporate Mary's philosophy of teaching and Martha's efficient methodologies. At the heart of our unit studies is the philosophy that God has created each of us with a unique personality, special gifts and different learning styles. God is the Creator of our children and of their faith! By incorporating a Mary heart at the center of our studies, we begin, progress and end with Jesus and the Bible as our focal point! We are free to be flexible with the curriculum we choose, the pace we progress, the topics we study and the order in which we learn. We can learn about topics that interest the children and we can learn them using their different learning styles. We can go faster if they understand, we can slow down if they need more help or we can flat out stop if the material is too hard. By using unit studies, we can connect all the humanities, sciences, and history altogether. We can study God's awesome HIStory and creation holistically. By studying this way, we can clearly see God's plan throughout history and His plan unfolding right before our eyes in modern times. And besides, it is fun too!

Radiating from the center, our Mary Philosophy, are all of Martha's methods and projects! Martha's methodologies are no nonsense and action-packed. Everyone needs to learn the basics! For the 3 R's we incorporate Martha's structure and diligent work ethic. Without reading, our children will not be able to read, understand, and apply God's Word. Without proficient writing skills, our children will not be able to effectively share the good news with others. And without mathematics, our children will not be able to solve problems and make sense of the world God has created. But Martha is also a hands-on kind of girl! In unit studies, we can learn and review the basics using a hands-on approach. We can integrate and incorporate the sciences, humanities, and history while learning and reinforcing the basic skills. As the expression goes, "All work and no play makes [Martha] a dull girl!" Using unit studies allows the flexibility to immerse ourselves in scientific inquiries and experiments, hands-on history projects, messy and down-right fun arts and craft ventures and hours and hours of reading those "I just can't put it down" kind of books! The Mary and Martha approach to unit studies complements any curriculum and enhances the learning styles of all involved in the process.

Plan the School Year

Once you have prayerfully chosen the "curriculum" you will use, spread it out on your bed. Take a day to pray over the material! Each year, my mother-in-law takes the kids for the day so I can plan and organize our school year. I pray over every book, every idea, and the calendar and I ask for God's guidance in the planning. I first break up the topics to be studied and decide what will be covered each month. Then I break down the month into four weeks and decide which specific skills will be addressed. As the year progresses, I then sit down each Saturday and figure the particular workbook pages we will cover, which books we will read, which experiments we will perform, which places we will visit, and which art projects we will attempt for that week. Before the school year begins, I usually choose the curriculum, arrange the topics to be studied and plan the first month of school.

Create a Schedule

Once I have an idea as to what will be studied and when, I sit down and create a schedule. (I use this term loosely!). Schedules stress me out! If I fall behind, I get nervous so I try to give myself some wiggle room. I write down time blocks and fill in the boxes with general topics.

SAMPLE

7:00-8:00	Wake up, do chores, brush teeth/hair, eat breakfast
8:00-10:00	Devotions, Reading, Spelling, Writing and Math
10:00- 11:00	Break! Morning Exercise
11:00-12:30	Projects- Science, Art, History, Game time
12:30-1:30	Lunch
1:30- 3:30	Play together, practice instruments, independent reading
3:30-5:30	Classes/ Activities/ Prepare dinner
5:30-6:30	Dinner
6:30-8:00	Family Time & Read Aloud
8:30	Bedtime Rituals- Sleep!

I know that on Wednesdays, my daughter has American Heritage Girls and Dance classes. On Mondays and Tuesdays my son has karate. On Thursday, we have violin lessons and on Tuesday evenings we have Bible Study at church. I write these weekly events on the schedule so that I plan accordingly on those days. For example, Wednesdays are a busy day so I don't plan any extra projects on that day. We make up for it on another day. Fridays are usually an activity-free day so I plan to play "catch-up" on that day. Any projects or assignments we didn't get to or finish during the week, the kids and I complete on Fridays. I leave it open specifically for that reason. For high schoolers, the morning or afternoon blocks can be adjusted to fit any outside accredited classes they may be taking.

Generate Lists

Once I have an outline of what topics will be covered and when during the year, I begin to create my lists! Remember, I am a Martha so I LOVE lists! However, I tend to be a slave to my "To Do List". I will let you in on a little secret of mine. I love checking off items on my "To Do List." I have even been known to add something to my list if I completed a task JUST so I could check it off! So needless to say, I function better with lists!

The first list I create is my yearly list. What will we need on a regular basis for the school year? Which books will we use daily or weekly? Which supplies will we need on a consistent basis? I use my yearly outline (or scope and sequence) to help guide the process. The items on this list tend to be books and materials we need for reading, writing, and mathematics and the supplies we need for art projects. (You can never have enough paper, index cards, paints, oil pastels and good-old- fashion Elmer's glue!) Once the list is created, I search the house. Before buying anything, I want to make sure I don't already have the materials needed or that we don't have supplies that can be recycled for the year.

Next, I study our plan for the first month of school. Which unit will we be studying? What kind of science experiments will we be performing? What kind of projects will we being doing? Which books will we be reading? Once again, I check the kitchen first for any science "equipment" and "chemicals" we will need. (I can find just about everything I need for a good basic chemistry set in my own kitchen!) I check the art closet and game armoire for supplies and possible "supplements" to our unit studies. I check our local library for books I want to read together. If the library doesn't have a particular book, I search for a similar title first. I check the Internet for kid-friendly, age appropriate websites that correlate to the desired topic. Then if all else fails, I either purchase the needed book or decide to not venture in that direction of our unit study.

Once my list of needed items is complete, I go shopping. I only buy what is on the list! It saves me time and money!

We are ready to start! I sit down each evening and write out my "To Do List" for the next day. My list includes everything from morning devotions to errands to specific schoolwork to chores that I would like to accomplish that day. I write them down, read a chapter or two of a good book and go to sleep! The next morning, I pray over my "To Do List". *"Trust in the Lord with all your heart, and lean not on your own understanding; in all your ways acknowledge Him, And He shall direct your paths"* (Proverbs 3: 5-6).

Prioritize and Simplify

I ask the Lord to direct my steps and to help me discern His agenda for my day. I ask Him for the wisdom to know what is of Him and what I am trying to accomplish in my own strength. If there is a particular problem that is bothering me, I ask Him for creative ideas to solve it or for the humility to lay it at His feet! My prayer over my to do list is "Not my will, Lord, but your will!" I don't' want to miss those precious teachable moments and I certainly don't want to miss those divine appointments He sends my way! I pray for the perseverance to do the "hard labor", the flexibility to get "off track" and the wisdom to know the difference. The Lord is so faithful! He clears my mind and helps me prioritize my list. I place the items at the top that absolutely need to be completed (devotions, pay the house mortgage, take a bath, call the dentist). Then I write the items that should be completed that day (particular school lessons, chores, fix dinner). At the bottom are the items I would like to accomplish this day but if they are not completed, they can wait till tomorrow (clean the bathroom, clean the bathroom, clean the bathroom). After praying over my to do list, there is a "peace that surpasses all understanding" that takes hold of my heart and mind! I know that *" I can do all things through Christ who strengthens me."* (Philippians 4:13)

Usually about this time, I am feeling a bit overwhelmed at the amount of topics on our yearly plan, lessons on our monthly plan and items on my daily to do list! So much to do, so little time! Periodically during the year (usually when I am feeling exhausted and overwhelmed again), I opt to P.A.S.S. Do you remember playing games as a kid that you could "Pass" if you didn't know the answer or if you didn't want to read aloud in class you could "Pass"? For me sometimes when my brain is on overload and I feel like there is not one more thing I can do, I just wish I could look at my husband and say, "Pass". (Sometimes I do and then I tip toe to the bedroom and take a long nap! I literally "pass" out!)

At the beginning of the year, do one more thing to organize and finalize your year of learning: P.A.S.S (Prioritize And Simplify, Sister!) I literally write down everything we do as a family, every activity or class the children participate in, and every responsibility I have at work and church. First, I prioritize the list. For example, church on Sunday mornings and Bible Study on Tuesday evenings are a MUST! Writing, grading papers and being a Sunday school teacher twice a month is a must! Family Night is a MUST!

Then I move on to the children's schedules. Sometimes I answer the phone or respond to an email as "Francesca's personal secretary. How may I help you?" My neighbor teases her all the time. "I thought you homeschooled! You are never home!" To that she just giggles and I slump with exhaustion! Does Francesca need to go to dance classes? Perform in the latest musical? Play the violin? Does Joseph have to go to swim lessons? Participate in gymnastics classes? The answer is of course NO! But does Francesca excel in the arts? Yes! Has God given her a passion for singing, dancing and acting? Yes! Does Joseph abound with energy and take to the water like a fish? Yes! Will they use their gifts for His glory later in life? I don't know but I am willing to give my children the opportunity to develop these gifts while they are young. I can't wait to sit back one day and watch how God will use them and their passions for His glory!

So with this in mind, we keep the dance classes (but not all three!) and we cart Francesca to rehearsals several months out of the year and we allow Joseph to practice his gymnastics moves on the sofa cushions and cart him to swim lessons every day for 8 weeks! Does

Francesca need to take voice lessons along side her violin lessons? No! Does Joseph need to be involved with year round soccer or spring *and* summer baseball leagues? No! So if the time is not right (or our checkbook), one, two or all are eliminated for a while.

Once the list is prioritized, I begin to pray and simplify the list and our lives! Francesca stopped piano for a whole year and she switched dance schools. Mainly because one school offered tap and jazz all in one class. What a difference that made in our schedule. Joseph opted to not do karate for a while if he could do swim lessons 5 days a week instead! I gave up teaching Sunday school every week and went to twice a month and I only teach twice a week at night as opposed to teaching in the afternoons 3-4 times a week.. These choices simplified our life (and saved on the gasoline bill as well!) Is there piano in Francesca's future? Quite possibly but not right now. Will Joseph play baseball? I am sure but he will have to wait till next season (or the season after that). Will I be a full time professor again? Who knows, it is in God's hands. But He is using my time at home (late at night I might add) to write and develop curriculum. The importance is to prioritize and to follow through on the simplifying! "Not my will but His will be done!"

Chapter 11
Organize Your Home

When I was in college, I couldn't study for finals unless my dorm room was immaculate. If the room was messy or there were errands that needed to be done, I couldn't concentrate! Luckily, God gave me a roommate who was a neat freak too! And she was never there so it was very quiet as well! I am still the same way! I can't think or write if the house is a mess! I can't concentrate if there are beds to be made and dishes to be cleaned. My surroundings have to be in order before I can buckle down on anything that requires me to think! I always go on a cleaning and reorganizing frenzy before we start school! It helps me think and refocus on the task at hand. My kids are normal kids so messy desks, cluttered bookshelves and crumpled papers don't seem to bother their concentration but it bothers me! So if they want their teacher's undivided attention, they know that certain things around the house have to be in order before we start "school".

In this section of the book, the neurotic Martha in me has a chance to come out! I want to share with you certain ideas and tasks I do that have helped simplify and organize our household. They have worked wonders for my family and for me! The projects given are just suggestions. Try some, ignore some, or save some for a later date!

The Notebook

Other than my Bible, the most important "book" in my life is my daily organizer. I didn't go out and buy one of those fancy ones although my husband loves his! I prefer an old fashion 3-subject spiral notebook! Noting fancy! I bring this notebook with me everywhere so it needs to be sturdy and durable! The first tab is labeled "Daily To Do List". The second tab is labeled "Lesson Plans" and the third tab is labeled "Long Term Projects". The infamous "To Do List" I mentioned earlier, finds its home in the first section of my notebook. Each day I write what needs to be accomplished (and what I would like to do) that day. See "Generate Lists" (page 62) for what goes on my list and how I pray over it each morning.

The second section, "Lesson Plans," is really just my "To Do List" for school each week. As discussed early in planning the school year, I schedule what will be taught each month. In my Lesson Plan section, I break down the month into weeks and list specifically what will be covered, what books will be read, what experiments will be preformed, etc. I list the days of the week and briefly record the details for each day.

SAMPLE:
Monday-
1. Read Genesis 1-3- Discuss creation, Sabbath and sin
2. Primary Language Lessons- pgs. 82-94
3. Review ½, ¼, 1/8 with Cuisenaire rods (Francesca) & ordinal numbers (Joseph's)
4. Write thank you letter to Grandma (Francesca) & numbers 1-7 (Joseph)
5. Acid & base experiments using cabbage juice, ph paper and turmeric sticks
6. Make collage of 7 days of creation
7. Draw or paint Garden of Eden
8. Read about Michelangelo and do art study of "Creation of Man" from the Sistine Chapel.
9. Add Adam & Eve and Michangleo to timeline.
10. Add summaries of Genesis 1-3 and life of Michelangelo into HIStory Notebook
11. Practice Violin
12. Wizard of Oz Rehearsal (5:30) and Karate (6:00)

Later that evening, I check off what was accomplished and what still needs to be done. I also use this as my official record for state authorities if we were ever to be challenge. The final section is where I record all those long-term projects I eventually need to tackle or I am dying to start. The curtains throughout the house desperately need to be taken down and washed. Both my daughter and I are allergic to house mites and dust so it is essential that this tedious chore get done. However, it doesn't need to be done weekly or even monthly. It just needs to get done. This is more of a spring-cleaning task. I have another book project I want to get started on, the kid's scrapbooks need to be up dated, and the summer vegetable garden needs to be planted before summer. All of these things are not necessities but they are things I need to do periodically or wish to do (at least monthly)! I am sure you have your own goals or pet projects that you could fill this section with. I am the taskmaster in the family so I usually place a date next to each item in the Long Term Projects list. It isn't a deadline per say, it is more of goal. If I have a date in mind, I can prioritize (and simplify) my Long Term List too! For example, next to cleaning curtains, I write October. (My daughter's allergy season begins in autumn and goes haywire in the winter months. So I try to do the curtains in October before her misery sets in!) Since my goal is to accomplish cleaning the curtains in October, I then begin to add "cleaning curtains" to my "Daily To Do List" in October. Eventually they are taken down, cleaned, ironed and put back up sometime in the month of October.

Family Calendar

Another necessity to smooth sailing in our home is incorporating a Family Calendar. Our family calendar is posted in the kitchen where all can see it, including my husband. It took a few years but I finally trained him to consult the calendar first before making any outside commitments for himself or the family. All classes, activities, special events, birthdays, anniversaries, and work schedules go on the Family Calendar! There are no excuses for missed birthdays any more. And because I am a visual learner, I tend to color code the calendar as well. Feel free to not take this extra step but it has helped me, a visual learner, tremendously. I write birthdays, anniversaries and special occasions in purple. (Purple is so festive!) I write my work schedule and my husband's meetings in red. (Red reminds me of being in debt therefore work is important!) I write regular classes in black (ballet, karate, violin, rehearsals, bible study, etc.) and other once a month special activities in blue (Date night, playdate with Lauren, parent meeting for homeschooling group, etc.) I save green for really out of the ordinary things like scrapbooking retreat or trip to Hawaii! (Green is my favorite color!) Make it a habit for everyone to check the family calendar before asking any questions or making any commitments!

Clutter Control

Now that we have our days organized, let's work on organizing our space! I married a pack rack and of course, I throw everything away! I am finding that my daughter has inherited the pack rat gene from her father! The amount of "stuff" that clutters up her room is amazing. What is even more mystifying is just how important each and every article is to her! I dare not throw anything away without asking!

If you are a pack rat like my daughter (and husband, father-in-law, and mother), then this section will be a bit challenging for you. But I know you can do it! First we need to find or purchase large plastic bins and retrieve a box of black plastic garbage bags. Why black you ask? I can't tell you how many times I have had my daughter's "clutter" under control, in the garbage bag and as I am walking out the door she screams, "NO! Wait! I need that notebook! It is my favorite!" The problem was she could see through the white plastic bag everything I was removing. So now, I use opaque, black, VERY large, plastic garbage bags.

To de-clutter, we need to apply the 5-bag rule! One bag is for throwing away, one bag is for recycling, one bag is for giving away, one bag is for storage, and one bag is for keeps! Use the black garage bags for "throw away" items. Use white plastic garbage bags for recyclables and give always. Use clear plastic bins for things you want to keep but put in storage. Use a bag, basket or bin for the items you need, want to keep but need to be placed into their proper space.

Pick a room! Any room will do! Personally, I start with the room that is the biggest eye soar for me! It is such a reward and a motivator to continue de-cluttering the rest of the house after one "mission impossible" is completed! Let's say you start in the kitchen. Round up all those lids that lost their bottoms and all those non-stick pans that destroy your pancakes every week. And those spices you haven't used since you moved in get rid of them. You can't use them and they don't work anymore so severe the relationship. Toss them in the throw away bag. Gather the mismatch mugs or bowls you haven't used in years and put them in the give away bag. Old cookbooks, broken measuring cups, and all those inkless pens, put them in the recycle bag. Do you have placemats you only use during the holidays that take up space in your kitchen drawers? Then put them in storage. While on the floor you may spot toys your son has been looking for under the cabinet. Place it in the "keepers" bin and save for later. You will need to put it back where it belongs (or your son will need to put these newly found items back where they belong!)

Don't stress over throwing things away. If you haven't used something in 2 years, either throw it away or give it away! It is just taking up valuable space. Don't throw away sentimental items or seasonal items, just put them in storage. Once you have successfully de-cluttered one room, pat yourself on the bag, take a break and devise your next plan of attack for a later day. A friend of mine says that she schedules 30 minutes a day to devote to things like this. She says it works for her. If you work better in short sessions, go for it! However, I get confused and stressed if I leave a project incomplete, especially when the de-cluttering job is cluttering my kitchen in the process. For major organizational projects like this, I like to save them for a day when I know I will have a few hours to devote to it. More is completed and I have a better sense of accomplishment at the end of the day.

One note about storage. After de-cluttering your home, you may find that in the process you cluttered your garage or storage unit. My husband and I use clear plastic bins for storage in the garage. We can see what is inside each bin and yes, you guessed it, I label the bins as well. This way, my husband can find the storage bin he needs quickly and effortlessly. For example, he places all of the sentimental baby bins (first shoes, favorite clothes, etc.) on the very top shelf. We have no reason to bring these down on a regular basis. He keeps seasonal items like Christmas decorations, all together but out of the way as well. School supplies that we may need once a month or so are kept on the lowest shelf. Seasonal clothes and shoes are kept in flat, plastic bins under our beds. Easy to get to and easy to put away!

Finally, we have eliminated much of our seasonal "knick knacks" from around the house and from storage as well. For me, it was too time consuming retrieving all of the decorations for an upcoming holiday, strategically placing them around the house, and then collecting and repacking all of the decorations when the holiday passed. Besides, the amount of dust the little stuffed bunnies, plastic eggs, colorful turkeys and patriotic do dads collected was unbearable! We decided a long time ago when our youngest was little and got into everything and the eldest child was diagnosed with a dozen or so allergies, that the cute (and usually breakable) knick-knacks had to go! We packed up all of our Christmas decorations and placed them into storage. Then I went through all of our other holiday decorations and kept sentimental, handmade or extremely cute (but small) items and then gave away, recycled or tossed out the rest. Now we have one storage box for all other seasonal decorations.

I missed decorating for an upcoming holiday or special occasion so I now use our centerpiece to commemorate seasons, units of study or special months. I change out the centerpiece once a month. I try to showcase something memorable that will be occurring that month. Sometimes, I use our centerpiece to showcase a unit of study we will be doing that month. For example in November, I decorate the center of the table with a beautiful table runner my mother-in-law gave me. On top of that I place several handmade "Thankful Turkeys" my children have made throughout the years. I also place a book of blessings in the center next to several autumn colored and scented votive candles. One year, my daughter made pilgrim stick puppets, which we placed in the centerpiece. Another year, she made wooden spool crosses with "Thank You, Jesus" written across them. These crosses found the place of honor in the midst of that year's centerpiece. I love fresh flower so I try to place a seasonal vase somewhere in the arrangement so that God's beautiful creation can enhance the table as well.

This year when we started our "time travel" from creation to Greeks, I used the centerpiece as a way to remind us daily of our studies that month. In a small frame a dear friend gave to me, I printed and framed Genesis 1:1 "In the beginning, God created the heavens and earth." I also printed up the creation story on art paper, rolled it up, burned the edges, left it outside for a few days and tied it with a piece of raffia. It looked very old and quite authentic. My daughter weaved a small basket from raffia (much like they did long ago) and my son pounded out a cross shape on a copper-type material. I placed these items in the center as well. I used a few other "old" looking vases, votive holders and plates to add to the authenticity of the centerpiece. As we sat down to do our school work at the table or when we gathered to break bread as a family, the centerpiece served as a reminder of what we were learning that month. It is a wonderful conversation starter for my husband when he sees something new added to the arrangement and it is a great witnessing tool to friends who come to visit! When asked about the centerpiece, the children bubble over with excitement (and information) about what our family is doing and learning.

The School Room

Whether you have a special room in the house for schoolwork or all learning takes place at the kitchen table, I find it helpful to designate a particular place (closet, bookshelf, etc) to house all of my school supplies. The office is where the computer and the majority of our bookshelves are found so this is the place I keep all of my "school stuff". I have a shelf for Francesca's "curriculum", a shelf for Joseph's "curriculum," a shelf for my homeschooling and devotional books and a whole bookcase (or two) of kid friendly books! This is where I keep our "book basket" as well. My husband got tired of library over due charges so now whenever we check out books at the library, they go in the very large "book basket". The kids know that when they want to read a library book they go to the basket to find it and when they are finished reading a library book they put it back into the "book basket". No missing books! No frantic searches before going to the library! I also designate one day a month for the library-Thursdays work best for us. This way, we check out all of our books at the same time and return them all at the same time! No mystery as to which book is due this week and which books we can keep for another week! Late fees have vanished from our home!

We also have a "unit basket" in our office. At the beginning of each month, I review what topics we will be studying. I search the house for every book that is related to the unit and place it in the "unit basket". It is a stress free and efficient way to have everything I need for the month at my fingertips! This way the only reason I need to go searching for a particular book is if I find we are going in a different direction than what was planned for the day!

Speaking of books, I also spend some time each summer reorganizing our bookshelves. This is something I put on my Long Term List. I try to organize the books according to subjects. One bookshelf has all of our non-fiction science, history, geography, and logical thinking puzzle books. Another bookshelf is lined with poetry, fiction novels, biographies and an abundance of art and music books. We also have a bookshelf filled with math-related picture books, math manipulatives and math games. One whole armoire is filled with nothing but games. My daughter's favorite books and authors are in her room and my son's favorite picture books are in his room. It takes a few hours to collect and reorganize all the books but it is well worth it during the year. The kids and I know exactly where to look for a particular topic, author or workbook!

Both of my children have desks in their room which are filled with paper, pencils, crayons, scissors, glue sticks, etc. So they always know where to look when a new project strikes their fancy! I have everything I need for the week's lessons on my desk in a neat pile. I hate piles but this is one pile that has order and meaning to it. On top of the pile is my Notebook with a tab strategically placed in the Lesson Plan section. I am not a slave to my "lesson plans" but I have a general idea as what should be accomplished that day and what items I will need to keep things moving smoothly.

My husband is the decorator in the family so papers hanging on the walls drive him a bit batty. So we designated the office as our "display room". He graciously placed several bulletin boards up in the office, built bookshelves and cleaned off surfaces so the kids and I could hang finished work, keep on going projects out in the open and the competed 3D displays have a place to call home! The printer, fax machine, copy machine and laptop computer are also in this room! It has made our life and homeschooling more enjoyable knowing that even though we cuddle on the sofa to read, work out math problems at the dining room table, perform our science experiments on the kitchen counter and create art projects on the outside patio, there is a place all of our "school stuff" can be found!

Space Savers

Everything has a space in our home! There is nothing more frustrating (and time consuming) than spending hours searching for something in the house. This can steal your joy very quickly. The kids learned early on that their toys and special collections belong in their rooms. We have baskets for everything and all around the house! In the living room, we have baskets under our coffee table filled with fun books to read and tons of train tracks. (This is the largest room in the house therefore it is the best room in the house for designing an awesome train line!) The kitchen has a fruit basket, onion and garlic basket, a recipe basket (I'll get to that in a minute) and a refrigerator magnet basket! At any given time, you can find whatever utensil, pot, container or spice you need in the kitchen. Now I am not saying that every drawer and cabinet is neatly organized and freshly lined with potpourri paper, but everything has a proper place in the kitchen. The kid friendly glasses and plates are stored in a lowest cabinet so the kids can reach them independently. (This saves me from a lot of unnecessary "serving"). The healthy, approved snacks are in two drawers that can easily be reached by the children. All they have to do is ask permission and then they can go get their own snack. The healthy refrigerated snacks are also in the bottom drawer of the refrigerator so that it is easy access for them as well!

We have a first aid basket in the master bathroom and a basket of hair do dads in the kid's bathroom. Each bedroom closet has shoe cubbies and a sock drawer. No need for endless searches of shoes (I am the worst at this one! I know there is a place for my shoes, but I always kick them off as soon as I walk into the door!) I collect teapots and my husband is a novice magician. I have my delicate collection in the Dining Room and my husband has his "secret" stash of tricks in the Living Room. My husband even converted an old water heater closet into our art supply room. He builds deep shelves from floor to ceiling in it. On the top shelf I keep old curriculum I used with Francesca that I am saving to use with Joseph. On the next shelf I put expensive art supplies and on the shelf that is eye level with the kids, are all of the supplies they use each day- glitter, glue, construction paper, felt, craft scissors, paint brushes, etc. The bottom shelf houses all of our science equipment in little boxes.

Even though the kids keep their toys in their room, there are baskets and shelves in there too. My son knows exactly where to look for his Legos, magnet-tiles, puzzles or toy cars at any given moment. (And he knows exactly where to put them when he is finished playing with them!). My daughter collects journals, purses, rocks and dolls. She too has a basket or shelf for each of her treasures. She knows where to find them and where to put them back!

We even have a closet that is used for all of the oversized products. My husband loves to shop at Costco. He insists he gets great deals. Even though this is true (and much appreciated) the problem still arises when he returns. Where do I put 36 rolls of toilet paper, 24 rolls of paper towels, 3 huge containers of animal crackers, plastic formless bags of cereal, cases of canned peas and carrots, and boxes and boxes of batteries? Where you ask? In the "Costco Closet". The overflow goes in this closet and out of the already bulging kitchen cabinets. And the best part is everyone knows were to go to find the roll of toilet paper when all is used up in the bathroom. One less problem I need to solve and one more thing my family can do independently! Life is good!

I would drive my family crazy and myself if I walked around all day picking up messes! So I save this "ritual" for later in the day. We do not go to bed without doing our daily "pick up" routine. The kids and I try to do this before Dad gets home but we are not always successful at this one. Many times, it happens as part of our bedtime ritual. If it was a good day, we put away our school stuff and art supplies when we finish our work. This way we only have toys and collections to round up and put away for the day. On really busy days, I walk around with yet another basket, a really big one, and collect from each room all of the items that do not belong in it and place them into their respective areas. Then the kids pitch in and help me clean and organize each room. My son knows he can keep his fire engines out in his room if I can walk from his door to his bed and my daughter knows her desk is her space! She doesn't have to clean it as long as she can find what she needs when she needs it!

Chores

Everyone has his or her own philosophy about chores! Some feel you should never pay your children to do their chores and others feel it is good training for the work force later in life. Whatever your philosophy is about rewards and consequences for chores, the fact remains when you homeschool, all should chip in! It is a matter of survival! You know the expression-"When Mama's happy, everyone's happy!" When my kids do their chores independently and they are done well, I am a happy camper! If they do them without being reminded, I am floating on cloud nine! Any home, especially if you homeschool is a happier (and cleaner) place when everyone pitches in and helps with the workload.

My children have their own daily chores. They need to make their beds, wash their hands and face, brush their teeth and hair, get dressed, and pick up their toys and dirty clothes. But they also have their weekly chores as well. On different days, my children are responsible for different chores. On Mondays, the kids vacuum. Francesca gets the large rooms and Joseph gets the smaller ones. On Tuesdays and Thursdays, Francesca is in charge of making lunch for all of us and Joseph sets the table. On Wednesdays and Fridays, Francesca sets the table and Joseph helps me prepare lunch. Fridays are garbage day. Francesca organizes the recyclables and Joseph helps collect the garage. Saturday is washday! My husband has taken over this job for me! (I love this guy!) The kids are responsible for putting their dirty clothes in the dirty hampers and helping my husband fold socks, towels and underwear. My husband does the washing, folding (and ironing) and I put everything away! My husband also washes the cars on Saturdays usually with one or both kids in tow.

I have kitchen duty and my husband (by his choice) has bathroom duty. (I know, he is an awesome man!) I cook the meals and I make a point of cleaning the kitchen after every meal. I found that if I left the dishes in the sink all day, the pile would be too hard to clean and the job would be too exhausting to do at the end of the day! So I clean as I go. The kids help clear the table. I clean the big pots and put the dishes and utensils in the dishwasher after every meal. After dinner, I clean the counter and table, dry the big pans and start the dishwashing machine. Of course a loaded dishwasher is waiting for me in the morning but I make a point of putting away all of the clean dishes before I start cooking breakfast the next day. My husband deep cleans the bathroom twice a month and we all wipe down the shower and sinks each day after we use them. Doing the little things throughout the day can be such time savers later on!

Cooking

Let's face it; we spend the majority of our waking hours in the kitchen! I thought I spent a lot of time in the kitchen when the kids were born but now that we homeschool, I feel like I am in the kitchen all day long! First there is breakfast. You need to cook it, eat it and clean it up. Then there is snack time! Then comes lunch. You need to prepare it, eat it and clean it up. Then snack time again! Finally comes dinner. You need to prepare it, cook it, eat it, and clean it up! No wonder my hands are dry and itchy!

Our family goes to the grocery once a week! If we forget something or run out of something, we make do! There is nothing worse and more time consuming then running to the market 2-3 times a week for a cartoon of milk or a loaf of bread. If we are missing a food item, we either do without or we improvise!

On Monday mornings, I plan our meals for the week and then survey the refrigerator and pantry for needed materials. You know me and lists! Yes, I have a master grocery list too! My master list is on the computer and it contains grocery items we usually buy on a weekly and monthly basis. On Mondays, I highlight all of the items we need for the week. If it is not highlighted, I know we still have an ample supply of it and I don't need to purchase it. (See the appendix for a sample list.) I have a column for "Others" and a column for "Dinner Menu". I write what we will be eating for dinner that week and then fill in the needed items in "Other" that we don't necessarily buy each week. For example, my family loves Eggplant Parmesan and Stuffed Artichokes but for obvious reasons, I do not cook this family favorite every week. Therefore eggplants and artichokes are not on my weekly list. However, bread crumbs, eggs, milk and tomato sauce are. I add the vegetables to the "Other" column and highlight the staples on the weekly list.

I also got tired of hearing my kids complain, "Peanut butter and Jelly sandwiches again!" So now I post the master grocery list on the refrigerator. Anything my children desire for the week, they are responsible for adding it to the list. Of course I have the "veto" option, but for the most part, if Francesca requests salami for the week and writes it on the list, I will get it at the grocery! If Joseph wants oatmeal instead of cream of wheat for the week and it is on the list, I will get it! No more complaining! If it is not on the list, I don't buy it!

I also have a "Recipe Basket". In this basket, I file weekly dinner menus. This basket has become a lifesaver! I never run around frantically searching for something to fix for dinner nor do I diligently start preparing dinner and find I don't have an important ingredient! I have devised 10 weekly menus, five summer/spring menus and five winter/fall menus. I do not plan for 7 meals in a week! I plan for 4 homemade dinners, two left over-nights and one sandwich night. Many times during the summer months, our sandwich nights become "eat out" evenings. I categorize the menus according to seasons due to the availability of seasonal fruits and vegetables. I don't want to plan a meal with asparagus and summer squash in the middle of winter. Nor do I want to make strawberry shortcake when fresh strawberries are not available.

On the outside of white letter-sized envelopes, I list the days of the week. Next to Sunday, I plan the most time consuming and favorite meal of the week. I try to make Sunday dinners special. And I usually need more time in the kitchen to prepare it! On Monday, I write "Soup" if it is winter/fall menus or "Salad" for spring/ summer menus. On Wednesday and Saturdays we have left overs and Friday is generally sandwich night! Next to Tuesday and Thursday, I write out a dinner menu.

SAMPLE- Spring/ Summer
Sunday - Chicken Parmesan, pasta, steamed green beans, salad, and garlic bread
Monday - Antipasto Pasta Salad (Cold)
Tuesday - Steak, Baked Potatoes, Corn on the Cob, salad
Wednesday - Left overs
Thursday - Grilled Salmon, Rice Pilaf, Steamed broccoli, dinner rolls
Friday - Sandwiches
Saturday - Left overs

Inside the envelope, I place any recipes I need for the week. For example, my family loves a hearty, Italian antipasto salad. To make sure I don't forget everyone's' favorite ingredients, I wrote our family recipe for Antipasto Salad and placed it in the week's envelope. I also make a list of the ingredients I will need that week in order to prepare the meals for that given week. When I print up my Master Grocery List for the week, I compare it to the ingredients on the menu list. I highlight or add to the Master List what I need to purchase for the week. I often get creative here as well. I have been known to use any white cheese I have for Chicken Parmesan! If we have strawberries in the garden but no tomatoes that week, we will have strawberries in our dinner salad instead of tomatoes! If we have left over salmon, I will make salmon salad instead of tuna fish salad for lunch the next day. If I am buying salami for the Antipasto Salad then guess what we are having for sandwich night? You guessed it- Salami!

In the "Recipe Basket", I also have an envelope for Easter, Christmas and Thanksgiving. My family looks forward to eating certain things on special holidays so I store these recipes in special envelopes. I also have envelopes just for desserts and appetizers for the days we entertain.. I also have a "berry" envelope which contains nothing but berry recipes! For the fall and winter I have a "pumpkin" envelope and an "apple" envelope. Inside, I can find any meal or treat prepared with apples or pumpkins! I am working on a banana envelope as we speak! My youngest hates fruit but he will eat anything with banana in it! I even have an "eggplant" envelope. If you haven't gathered by now, my family is a big fan of eggplant. I have collected so many recipes that I need a special envelope in which to store them.

Yes, it took me a while to put together this "recipe basket"! But now, our meals for the week are planned, my grocery lists are complete and it is all right at my fingertips. No thinking required! When I want to treat the family with a special dessert, I can look through the envelope files for just the right one. If we went apple picking and have bushels of apples to eat, I flip through my apple envelope for ideas. I do have a few cookbooks, but a few years ago I went through and gave away all of the cookbooks I hadn't used in over a year. I kept my favorites and placed them on the shelf next to my recipe basket. When I am in the mood to try something new, I open one of my tried and true cookbooks (or I surf the net!) Spending the time to organize the kitchen and create my "recipe basket" has proven to be invaluable! The kids know what we will be eating and I know what I will be cooking. It has cut down on the fast food and has given me back more time to spend with my family!

Martha's Projects:

1. Buy a 3-ring notebook and label each section. Brainstorm all of the things you would like to start or finish this year. Write them in the "Long Term Project" section. Before you go to bed, write down in the "To Do List" section all of the things you need to accomplish tomorrow. And just for fun, brainstorm a few fun projects to do with your children this week for school. Record them in the "Lesson Plan Section."

2. Pick one room in your house that you will "de-clutter". Tell the family and encourage everyone to help!

3. Using the template in the Appendix, create your own Master Grocery List and use it this week! Pick out 4 of your favorite recipes and organize them in an envelope. You are now one step closer to creating your very own "Recipe Basket".

4. Pick the busiest day you had this week. List EVERYTHING you did and when. Prayerfully consider how to reorganize your day into a doable and stress-free day. Then write a tentative school/chore schedule for you and your family. Try it out sometime this week.

5. Discuss with your husband the chores that need to be completed daily and weekly. Decide together which chores you will give to the children and which chores can be done monthly instead of weekly.

Chapter 12
Conclusion

But as for me and my family, we will serve the LORD."
Joshua 24:15

Details, details, details! I am a planner! I see the big picture! I have tons of ideas as to how a certain project should look or how a particular unit should progress. I am full of energy and excitement when a new project or unit begins! I can't wait to see how it will turn out! However, I am lacking in the follow thru department. While in the midst of a new unit or project, my mind becomes engrossed in the new ideas floating around in my head. I tend to slack on the details of a current project because I am too busy formulating the plans for the next one! I guess this is why I love starting a new book and I despise the final stages of production. It is all about details!

However, our God, the Creator, is a man of details! When creating the world in which humans would live, Creator God made sure life and life in abundance would be made possible, right down to the precise distance of the earth from sun, the amount of cloud covering in the atmosphere and the delicate process of photosynthesis to recycle the carbon dioxide being produced.

When God, our Father, gave Noah the command to build the ark

His instructions were detailed and his measurements were precise. When God, our Savior, instructed Moses and the Israelites to build the tabernacle, His directives were detailed down to what metals and woods should be used. And when Solomon began to build the temple in Jerusalem, God, our King, laid out the precise dimensions and detailed description of how the temple should look and be used. The Master Architect was involved in the building process and was concerned with every little detail.

We have come to the end of our building process and now our rooms are finally clean and reorganized. We can raise our hands and lift our eyes up to Jesus and know with full confidence that God has a master plan for you and for me and for our children! *"For I know the plans I have for you," declares the Lord, "plans to prosper you and not to harm you, plans to give you hope and a future"* (Jeremiah 29:11). He has plans to prosper our children, plans to give them a future full of hope! As we build a homeschool, one room at a time, we can rest assure that God is in control of our building process and He will take care of the details. Our families, our home and our lessons will prosper if we educate our children with Mary's philosophy. If our devotion for Jesus and our love for God's Word are at the core of our home and our homeschool, then indeed our children's future will be one of hope.

On the flip side, our children, home and curriculum will prosper if we teach our children using Martha's methodologies. If we conscientiously and diligently teach our children according to the different learning styles God has placed within them, then our children will indeed use their gifts and talents for God's glory. *"However, as it is written: 'No eye has seen, no ear has heard, no mind has conceived what God has prepared for those who love him' "* (1 Corinthians 2:9).

It is my prayer that you and I will build our homeschool, one room at a time, in such a way that our children will have a heart for God. And then when they grow and have their own families that they in turn will build a home for Jesus Christ! Joshua summed it up best: *"But as for me and my family, we will serve the LORD"* (Joshua 24:15). May God richly bless your homeschool adventure for His glory!

Appendix A:
A Mom's Job Description

Job Description:

Long term, team players needed, for challenging permanent work in an, often chaotic environment. Candidates must possess excellent communication and organizational skills and be willing to work variable hours, which will include evenings and weekends and frequent 24 hour shifts on call. Some overnight travel required, including trips to primitive camping sites on rainy weekends and endless sports tournaments in far away cities. Travel expenses not reimbursed. Extensive courier duties also required.

Responsibilities:

The rest of your life. Must be willing to be hated, at least temporarily, until someone needs $5. Must be willing to bite tongue repeatedly. Also, must possess the physical stamina of a pack mule and be able to go from zero to 60 mph in three seconds flat in case, this time, the screams from the backyard are not someone just crying wolf. Must be willing to face stimulating technical challenges, such as

101

small gadget repair, mysteriously sluggish toilets and stuck zippers. Must screen phone calls, maintain calendars and coordinate production of multiple homework projects. Must have ability to plan and organize social gatherings for clients of all ages and mental outlooks. Must be willing to be indispensable one minute, an embarrassment the next. Must handle assembly and product safety testing of a half million cheap, plastic toys, and battery operated devices. Must always hope for the best but be prepared for the worst. Must assume final, complete accountability for the quality of the end product. Responsibilities also include floor maintenance and janitorial work throughout the facility.

Possibility For Advancement & Promotion:

Virtually none. Your job is to remain in the same position for years, without complaining, constantly retraining and updating your skills, so that those in your charge can ultimately surpass you.

Previous Experience:

None required unfortunately. On-the-job training offered on a continually exhausting basis.

Wages, Compensation and Benifits:

None. You pay them, offering frequent raises, bonuses and the occasional bribe. A balloon payment is due when they turn 18 because of the assumption that college will help them become financially independent. When you die, you give them whatever is left. While no health or dental insurance, no pension, no tuition reimbursement, no paid holidays and no stock options are offered. The oddest thing about this reverse-salary scheme is that you actually enjoy it and wish you could only do more. This job supplies limitless opportunities for personal growth and free hugs for life if you play your cards right.

Appendix B:
Recommended Reading

Chapter 2: Foundation

Strobel, Lee (1998). *The Case for Christ: A Journalist's Personal Investigation of the Evidence for Jesus*

---- (2000). *The Case for Faith: A Journalist Investigates the Toughest Objections to Christianity*

Chapter 3: The Living Room

George, Elizabeth (1997). *A Woman's Walk with God*

Jensen, (2002), *Praying God's Attributes*

Maxwell, Teri (2001). *Homeschooling with a Meek and Quiet Spirit*

Homeschool Encouager.com

Chapter 4: The Dining Room

Hunt, Gladys (2002) *Honey for a Child's Heart*

Chapter 5: The Study

Andreola, Karen (2001). *Pocketful of Pinecones: Nature Study With the Gentle Art of Learning : A Story for Mother Culture*

Clarkson, C. & Clarkson, S. (2001). *Educating the Wholehearted Child Revised & Expanded*

Tobias, Cynthia U. (1998). *The Way They Learn*

Waring, Diana. (1996). *Beyond Survival: A Guide to Abundant-Life Homeschooling*
.

Chapter 8: The Bedroom

Omartian, Stormie (1997). *The Power of a Praying Wife*

Chapter 9: The Bathroom

Munger, Robert B. (1992). *My Heart-Christ's Home: A Story for Old & Young*

Chapter 10: Spring Cleaning

Maxwell, Steven (2000). *Managers of Their Homes: A Practical Guide to Daily Scheduling for Christian Homeschool Families.*

Titus 2.com

Appendix C:
Grocery Master List

Eggs
Bread
Milk
Chocolate Soy Milk
Butter
Yogart
Sour Cream
Deli Meat
Juice
Bananas
Apples
Celery
Lettuce
Veggie
Veggie
Other fruit
Mushrooms
Potatoes
Sweet Potatoes
Onions

Garlic
Tomato Sauce
Parmesan Cheese
Mozzarella Cheese (shredded)
Monterrey Jack Cheese (shredded)
American slice Cheese
String Cheese
Tuna fish
Rice
Sugar
Salt
Mayo
Mustard
Ketchup
Jelly
Peanut Butter
Sweet Relish
Muffin Mix
Other
Dinner Menu

Printed in the United States
101062LV00005B/1-3/A

9 781432 701260